THE
GOSPEL OF
LUKE:
DISPENSATIONALLY CONSIDERED

A GRACE EXPOSITIONAL COMMENTARY

Dr. David Alan Greene

GRACEWORD PUBLISHING

Contents

To B'nai Avraham — the children of Abraham

Now I say that
Jesus Christ
was a minister of the circumcision
for the truth of God,
to confirm the promises
made unto the fathers:

– The Apostle Paul

Acknowledgements

I would like to express a special thanks to Jon and Susan McMahon and Frances Greene for their continued encouragement. To those who assisted with the preparation of this book, I offer my gratitude.

Introduction

Dear reader if you have read some of my other commentaries on the gospels, you will note that the Introductions are very similar. The introduction plays a key role in understanding the material presented. The reader should be familiar with the concept and application of rightly dividing the Word of Truth. It is also known as the dispensational approach to Scripture. To summarize: God ordered the Bible by dividing it into ages or dispensations. Each of these divisions were intended to lead towards His ultimate goal of restoring His Creation.

Traditionally, the Bible has been divided into seven ages or periods of time. Sometimes, these divisions are referred to as administrations in which God makes Himself known. There is a progression in these administrations which leads to its conclusion. Jumping into the middle of a book or movie series does not allow the reader to fully understand or enjoy the series in full. GraceWord Publishing has created the Grace Expositional Bible Commentary.

Each of the books included in the series walks the reader through the biblical book verse-by-verse. As this is done, it applies a system or method of interpretation.

For this reason, I recommend the reader be familiar with the simple concept of "rightly dividing" the Word of Truth. Paul instructed his student, Timothy, in 2 Timothy 2:15:

> 15 **Study to shew thyself approved unto God, a workman that needeth not to be ashamed, <u>rightly dividing the word of truth</u>.**

To understand any portion of Scripture, it must be seen within it proper division. It is dangerous to take verses of Scripture out of its context. Doing so will increase the risk of missing the point entirely or misunderstanding to whom the text was intended.

Like the number of days that God took to create the earth, I believe there are seven periods of time or ages or dispensations that He will take to redeem His Creation. The Gospel of Luke opens in the middle of the fifth dispensation which is the Age of Law. The Jews received the Law from Moses after God used him to lead His people out of Egypt. It was in the Wilderness that God created Israel to be a "peculiar" or special people. They are to be a holy nation separated from all the other nations. Israel has a purpose!

God told Moses to speak to Israel. Exodus 19:6:

> 6 **And ye shall be unto me <u>a kingdom of priests, and an holy nation</u>. These are the words which thou shalt speak unto the children of Israel.**

This was God's ultimate purpose for Israel. They will play a key role in His restored Creation.

Mosaic Covenant

Through Moses, God offered the children of Abraham, Isaac, and Jacob a binding contract or covenant. It would contractually bind God and His people. In the verses that follow, notice the offer and the acceptance. The people bound themselves to this conditional agreement. Verses 7-8:

> 7 **And Moses came and called for the elders of the people, and laid before their faces all these words which the LORD commanded him.**

> 8 <u>**And all the people answered together,**</u>

**and said, All that the LORD hath spo-
ken we will do. And Moses returned the
words of the people unto the LORD.**

This agreement or covenant remains in effect even to
this day. This fact is important. Nothing has changed
for the Jews since the day they voluntarily accepted
the terms of this agreement. God has not voided this
covenant in spite of Israel's actions.

This means that the Law remained in full effect
throughout Jesus' earthly ministry. Consider His
words in the Sermon of the Mount. A multitude of
Jews gathered to hear Him speak. Matthew 5:17-18:

> 17 **Think not that I am come to destroy
> the law, or the prophets: I am not come
> to destroy, but to fulfil.**
>
> 18 **For verily I say unto you, Till heaven
> and earth pass, one jot or one tittle shall
> in no wise [way] pass from the law, till
> [until it] all be fulfilled.**

So, the Law will be fulfilled at the end of the restoration. Jesus Christ is the One Who fulfills the Law.

Even after His death and resurrection, those
who followed his Gospel of the Kingdom remain

bound to the Law. Later in the book of James, the Apostle James wrote to the children of Abraham as they await the return of their Messiah. Look how he addresses his letter which was sent to comfort and encourage the Kingdom Believers. James 1:1:

> 1 **James, a servant of God and of the Lord Jesus Christ, <u>to the twelve tribes which are scattered abroad, greeting</u>.**

Knowing to whom James wrote this letter reveals something important. It becomes clear that the Law is still in effect for the Jews who follow the Gospel of the Kingdom. James, who was one of the Twelve, wrote this in verse 2:10:

> 10 **For whosoever shall keep the whole law, and yet [but] offend in one point, he is guilty of all.**

He is reminding them of their obligation according to the Mosaic Covenant. The entire Law was read aloud to those in the Wilderness as it is read to the congregation every year. Consider, again, their response. Exodus 19:8:

> 8 **And all the people answered together, and said, <u>All that the LORD hath spo-</u>**

ken we will do. **And Moses returned the words of the people unto the LORD.**

Notice it is not "some" of what God said, but "all" of what God said to them. The first five books of the Bible are called the "books of Moses." In the fifth book, Deuteronomy, there was a portion of the Mosaic Covenant which is referred to as the "blessings and curses." From this, it is clear that this covenant is conditional. IF they obey and do what is right according to the covenant, THEN God will bless them. However, IF they break one point of the covenant, THEN God will curse or punish them. James reiterated this point in his letter to them. He reminds them of their commitment to this lasting covenant.

Since evidence speaks louder that opinion, here are two portions from Deuteronomy 28. The following refers to the blessings. Verses 1-2:

> 1 **And it shall come to pass, if thou shalt hearken diligently unto the voice of the LORD thy God, to observe and to do all his commandments which I command thee this day, that the LORD thy God will set thee on high above all nations of the earth:**

> 2 **And all these blessings shall come on**

thee, and overtake thee, if thou shalt hearken unto the voice of the LORD thy God.

However, if they fail to keep the Law in its entirety, then there would be punishment. Verse 15:

15 **But it shall come to pass, if thou wilt not hearken unto the voice of the LORD thy God, to observe to do all his commandments and his statutes which I command thee this day; that all these curses shall come upon thee, and overtake thee:**

In both references, the word "all" plays a key part in the effect it will have upon the children of Abraham, Isaac, and Israel.

From Moses, to King David, to all the Old Testament prophets, the Law of Moses was in effect. Nothing had changed when Jesus was born. The Apostle Paul explains that Jesus was under the Law and His purpose was to redeem those who were under the Law. Galatians 4:4-5:

4 **But when the fulness of the time was come, God sent forth his Son, made of a woman, made under the law, 5 To**

**redeem them that were under the law,
that we might receive the adoption of
sons.**

There are two other covenants in the Old Testament that will have an impact on the people in the Gospel of Luke. In addition to the Mosaic Covenant, other covenants were made with Abraham and King David. The Jews were taught well and they knew their Scripture. It gave them hope for the future because they had faith that God would fulfill them. These two covenants are unconditional. This means that God will fulfill these covenants regardless of Israel's actions. Here, they are summarized:

Abrahamic Covenant:

The following is found in Genesis 12:1-3:

**1 Now the LORD had said unto Abram,
Get thee out of thy country, and from
thy kindred, and from thy father's
house, unto a land that I will shew thee:**

**2 And I will make of thee a great nation,
and I will bless thee, and make thy
name great; and thou shalt be a blessing:**

3 And I will bless them that bless thee, and curse him that curseth thee: and in thee shall all families of the earth be blessed.

Davidic Covenant:

God told the prophet Nathan to deliver this message to King David. 2 Samuel 7:12-13:

12 And when thy days be fulfilled, and thou shalt sleep with thy fathers, <u>I will set up thy seed after thee</u>, which shall proceed out of thy bowels, <u>and I will establish his kingdom.</u>

13 He shall build an house for my name, and <u>I will stablish the throne of his kingdom for ever.</u>

The Seed or Son of David is Jesus Christ. Verses 14-16:

14 <u>I will be his father, and he shall be my son</u>. If he commit iniquity, I will chasten him with the rod of men, and with the stripes of the children of men:

15 But my mercy shall not depart away

from him, as I took it from Saul, whom I put away before thee.

16 **And thine house and thy kingdom shall be established for ever before thee: thy throne shall be established for ever.**

I believe knowing these facts adds a deeper understanding of the Word of Truth. For the more advanced student, you may wish to consider reading *Letters To Theophilus: Are You Ready For The End Times?* and *The Glorious Destiny of Israel: The Fulfillment of God's Promises and Prophecies to Israel.* These two books present "two sides of the same coin" from the perspective of both the non-Jew and Jew respectively. Others may enjoy reading an overall summary of the Bible found in *The Hidden Gospel: Once Hidden But Now Revealed.* It highlights key events in the Bible and explains how it all comes together in the end. Some are available on audiobooks.

It is my hope that people will learn, understand, and enjoy their Bible.

1

About the Apostle Luke

Luke is the author of both the Gospel of Luke and the Acts of the Apostles. He does not address them to a specific group of people as do the later epistles. Instead, he addresses them to "Theophilus." Many have tried to identify an individual. There is no mention of that name in any other writing. I do not believe that it is an individual, but rather a collective name since "Theophilus" means "one who loves God." This would be anyone who loves God and desires to learn more about Jesus Christ and God's work. His narration of the birth of Christ is the one most often read aloud in assemblies as they celebrate the birth of Christ.

Luke's extensive knowledge of the Greek language and his ability to write indicate that he was highly educated. We also know that Luke was a doctor. Paul refers to him as the "beloved physician"

(Col. 4.4). This fact helps to explain the accuracy and detail that he used in his writing. It is believed that Luke was Grecian, but this does not mean that he was a Gentile. Some scholars have debated as to whether Luke was a Jew or a Gentile. Paul honors the Jews because God entrusted to them the words of God. Writing to the Gentiles, the Apostle Paul wrote, "What advantage then hath the Jew? or what profit is there of circumcision? Much [in] every way: chiefly, because that unto them were committed the oracles of God" (Rom. 3:1-2).

Luke was not part of the Twelve. However, it is believed that he was one of the Seventy who were chosen by Jesus to declare the good news that the kingdom of God was at hand. Luke 10:1; 9:

> 1 **After these things <u>the Lord appointed other seventy</u> also, and sent them two and two before his face into every city and place, whither he himself would come.**

> 9 **And heal the sick that are therein, and say unto them, <u>The kingdom of God is come nigh [near] unto you.</u>**

Besides the reference by Paul to Luke being a physician, there is one other reference to him being with

Paul before his execution. Paul writes, "Only Luke is with me . . ." (2 Tim. 4:11). Luke had been a companion of Paul on his missionary journeys. However, since he is the writer of Acts, he included himself by using "we" as a pronoun. We can find evidence of this in Acts 16, 20, 21, 27, and 28.

It is believed that Luke died at 84 at Thebes in present-day Greece in the late first century. During his life, he made a significant contribution to the New Testament writings. His two books alone comprises over twenty-seven percent of its content while the Apostle Paul contributed twenty-three percent. Between them, they wrote over fifty percent of the New Testament.

2

Luke 1 (Part I)

Luke sought out and collected the accounts of various eyewitnesses who saw and heard Jesus during His earthly ministry. These testimonies he compiled and recorded them into his gospel. Luke 1:1-4:

1 Forasmuch as many have taken in hand to set forth in order a declaration of those things which are most surely believed among us,

2 Even as they delivered them unto us, which from the beginning were eyewitnesses, and ministers of the word;

3 It seemed good to me also, having had perfect understanding of all things from the very first, to write unto thee in order, most excellent Theophilus,

4 That thou mightest know the certainty of those things, wherein thou hast been instructed.

The king who ruled over Judaea was King Herod I who was also known as Herod the Great. Zacharias was a priest who served at the Temple. The Temple was in full operation and the priests there served in a "course" which is like a deployment. They worked in "shifts" for the prescribed period of time while living at the Temple. Verses 5-9:

5 There was in the days of Herod, the king of Judaea, a certain priest named Zacharias, of the course of Abia: and his wife was of the daughters of Aaron, and her name was Elisabeth.

6 And they were both righteous before God, walking in all the commandments and ordinances of the Lord blameless. 7 And they had no child, because that Elisabeth was barren, and they both were now well stricken in years.

8 And it came to pass, that while he executed the priest's office before God in the order of his course, 9 According to the custom of the priest's office, his lot

was to burn incense when he went into the temple of the Lord.

The Temple operated twenty-four hours a day and its doors were never closed unless there was a dire situation. Gabriel is the angel who delivered the response from God to the prophet Daniel. Now, he was dispatched to bring the following news to Zacharias. Verses 10-14:

> 10 **And the whole multitude of the people were praying without at the time of incense.** 11 **And there appeared unto him an angel of the Lord standing on the right side of the altar of incense.**
>
> 12 **And when Zacharias saw him, he was troubled, and fear fell upon him.** 13 **But the angel said unto him, Fear not, Zacharias: for thy prayer is heard; and thy wife Elisabeth shall bear thee a son, and thou shalt call his name John.** 14 **And thou shalt have joy and gladness; and many shall rejoice at his birth.**

Gabriel spoke about his son whose coming was foretold. He will be "the voice of him that crieth in the wilderness, Prepare ye the way of the LORD . . ." (Isa. 40:3). Verses 15-17:

15 For he shall be great in the sight of the Lord, and shall drink neither wine nor strong drink; and <u>he shall be filled with the Holy Ghost</u>, even from his mother's womb. **16** <u>And many of the children of Israel shall he turn to the Lord their God</u>.

17 And he shall go before him in the spirit and power of Elias, to turn the hearts of the fathers to the children, and the disobedient to the wisdom of the just; to make ready a people prepared for the Lord.

Later, His disciples ask Jesus if Elijah would come before His Coming at the end of the age. Jesus responds by saying that John the Baptist came "before him in the spirit and power of Elias" who is Elijah.

The greatness of God is revealed in the weakness of His people. Like Abraham and Sarah, it was God Who gave them the miracle of a son while they were late in years. God was now doing the same thing for Zacharias and Elisabeth. Verses 18-19:

18 And Zacharias said unto the angel, Whereby shall I know this? for I am an old man, and my wife well stricken in

years. 19 **And the angel answering said unto him, I am Gabriel, that stand in the presence of God; and am sent to speak unto thee, and to shew thee these glad tidings.**

Lack of faith in the Word of God is an insult to God. Zacharias did not believe the angel and the delay caused attention in the Temple. Verses 20-22:

20 **And, behold, thou shalt be dumb, and not able to speak, until the day that these things shall be performed, because thou believest not my words, which shall be fulfilled in their season.**

21 **And the people waited for Zacharias, and marvelled that he tarried so long in the temple.** 22 **And when he came out, he could not speak unto them: and they perceived that he had seen a vision in the temple: for he beckoned unto them, and remained speechless.**

Zacharias received the announcement of the birth of his son who would be the herald of God's Son.

After his allotted time of service, Zacharias returned home to his wife. Verse 23:

23 And it came to pass, that, as soon as the days of his ministration [service] were accomplished, he departed to his own house.

However, because of her advanced age, Elisabeth hid her pregnancy from the public. Verses 24-25:

24 And after those days his wife Elisabeth conceived, and hid herself five months, saying, **25** Thus hath the Lord dealt with me in the days wherein he looked on me, to take away my reproach among men.

Meanwhile, there was another major event happening. It was the announcement to Mary, an unmarried woman, that she would also have a Son. Verses 26-28:

26 And in the sixth month the angel Gabriel was sent from God unto a city of Galilee, named Nazareth, **27** To a virgin espoused to a man whose name was Joseph, of the house of David; and the virgin's name was Mary.

28 And the angel came in unto her, and said, Hail, thou that art highly favoured, the Lord is with thee: blessed art thou among women.

We can understand why this may be troubling to a young woman especially one who has never been with a man. Verses 29-33:

29 And when she saw him, she was troubled at his saying, and cast in her mind what manner of salutation this should be. 30 And the angel said unto her, Fear not, Mary: for thou hast found favour with God.

31 And, behold, thou shalt conceive in thy womb, and bring forth a son, and shalt call his name JESUS. 32 He shall be great, and shall be called the Son of the Highest: and the Lord God shall give unto him the throne of his father David:

33 And he shall reign over the house of Jacob for ever; and of his kingdom there shall be no end.

We are going to pause here for a moment. I would like you to see how this all ties together.

After the Fall, God pronounced a curse on Satan and discloses exactly Who will crush him. Genesis 3:14-15:

> **14 And the LORD God said unto the serpent, Because thou hast done this, thou art cursed above all cattle, and above every beast of the field; upon thy belly shalt thou go, and dust shalt thou eat all the days of thy life:**

> **15 And <u>I will put enmity between thee and the woman, and between thy seed and her seed</u>; it shall bruise thy head, and thou shalt bruise his heel.**

Wait! Whose seed did God say? This is important. The sin of man is transferred through the male. However, God interceded and gave this Seed directly to the woman making it "her seed." The transmission of guilt and curse from the original sin was not transferred to Mary! Add to this the sinless life of Jesus and you have the sinless Lamb of God. This singular event ties the events in Genesis and Revelation together! The Apostle Paul wrote in 1 Corinthians 15:21-22:

> **21 For since by man came death, by man came also the resurrection of the dead.**

22 For as in Adam all die, even so in Christ shall all be made alive.

Now, we can return to our text. Luke 1:34-37:

34 Then said Mary unto the angel, How shall this be, seeing I know not a man?

35 And the angel answered and said unto her, The Holy Ghost shall come upon thee, and the power of the Highest shall overshadow thee: therefore also that holy thing which shall be born of thee shall be called the Son of God.

36 And, behold [be it known], thy cousin Elisabeth, she hath also conceived a son in her old age: and this is the sixth month with her, who was called barren.

37 For with God nothing shall be impossible.[!]

Here is Mary's response to the angel. Verse 38:

38 And Mary said, Behold the handmaid of the Lord; be it unto me according to thy word. And the angel departed from her.

For propriety, Mary decided to keep the matter private and acted on the angel's suggestion. She would move in with her cousin who was also pregnant. Concerning John, we are told that "he shall be filled with the Holy Ghost, even from his mother's womb" (v. 15). Mary arrives at the home of Zacharias and Elisabeth. Verses 39-45:

> 39 And Mary arose in those days, and went into the hill country with haste, into a city of Juda; 40 And entered into the house of Zacharias, and saluted Elisabeth.

> 41 And it came to pass, that, when Elisabeth heard the salutation of Mary, the babe leaped in her womb; and Elisabeth was filled with the Holy Ghost: 42 And she spake out with a loud voice, and said, Blessed art thou among women, and blessed is the fruit of thy womb.

> 43 And whence [how] is this to me, that the mother of my Lord should come to me? 44 For, lo, as soon as the voice of thy salutation sounded in mine ears, the babe leaped in my womb for joy.

> 45 And blessed is she that believed: for

there shall be a performance of those things which were told her from the Lord.

Mary was overwhelmed with joy that God had chosen her to bear His Son and Elisabeth confirmed it. What follows is referred to as Mary's Magnificat or the Song of Mary. It encapsulated her praises to God. Verses 46-55:

46 And Mary said, My soul doth magnify the Lord, 47 And my spirit hath rejoiced in God my Saviour. 48 For he hath regarded the low estate of his handmaiden: for, behold, from henceforth all generations shall call me blessed.

49 For he that is mighty hath done to me great things; and holy is his name. 50 And his mercy is on them that fear him from generation to generation.

51 He hath shewed strength with his arm; he hath scattered the proud in the imagination of their hearts.

52 He hath put down the mighty from their seats, and exalted them of low degree. 53 He hath filled the hungry with

good things; and the rich he hath sent empty away.

54 He hath holpen [has helped] his servant Israel, in remembrance of his mercy; 55 As he spake to our fathers, to Abraham, and to his seed for ever.

This is a wonderful hymn of praise from the lips of Jesus' mother.

Here again, we will hit pause. Many Gentiles follow a religion built upon the belief that Jesus came to save the Gentiles. The Apostle Paul makes a statement to the Gentiles, "Now I say that Jesus Christ was a minister of the circumcision for the truth of God, to confirm the promises made unto the fathers" (Rom. 15:8). Now, let us tie this together. Note particularly the use of the word "fathers" as it pertain to Israel in this verse. God is sending help to His servant Israel. He has remembered His mercy which He had spoken "to our fathers, to Abraham, and to his seed for ever" (v. 55). Therefore, God is confirming that He will fulfill "the promises" He made to Abraham, Isaac, Jacob, and King David.

God is faithful to keep His promises and He should never be doubted. We will continue with the remainder of Luke 1 in the next chapter.

16

3

Luke 1 (Part II)

Mary, pregnant with Jesus, stayed with Elisabeth until she gave birth to John. Luke 1:56-66:

56 And Mary abode [lived] with her about three months, and returned to her own house. 57 Now Elisabeth's full time came that she should be delivered; and she brought forth a son.

58 And her neighbours and her cousins heard how the Lord had shewed great mercy upon her; and they rejoiced with her.

59 And it came to pass, that on the eighth day they came to circumcise the child; and they called him Zacharias, after the name of his father.

60 And his mother answered and said, Not so; but he shall be called John. 61 And they said unto her, There is none of thy kindred that is called by this name. 62 And they made signs to his father, how he would have him called.

63 And he asked for a writing table, and wrote, saying, His name is John. And they marvelled all. 64 And his mouth was opened immediately, and his tongue loosed, and he spake, and praised God.

65 And fear came on all that dwelt round about them: and all these sayings were noised abroad throughout all the hill country of Judaea.

66 And all they that heard them laid them up in their hearts, saying, What manner of child shall this be! And the hand of the Lord was with him.

Having his tongue now loosed, Zacharias burst forth with words of praise. His son was called to be the prophet of the Most High. He would be the one to announce the arrival of the Messiah, the Son of God. Here are the words of his praises. Verses 67-79:

67 And his father Zacharias was filled with the Holy Ghost, and prophesied, saying,

68 Blessed be the Lord God of Israel; for he hath visited and <u>redeemed</u> his people, 69 And hath raised up <u>an horn of salvation for us in the house of his servant [King] David;</u>

70 As he [God] spake by the mouth of his holy prophets, which have been since the world began: 71 That we should be saved from our enemies, and from the hand of all that hate us;

72 <u>To perform the mercy promised to our fathers, and to remember his holy covenant;</u> 73 <u>The oath which he sware to our father Abraham,</u>

74 That he would grant unto us, that we being delivered out of the hand of our enemies might serve him without fear, 75 <u>In holiness and righteousness before him, all the days of our life.</u>

76 And thou [John], [my] child, shalt be called the prophet of the Highest: for

thou shalt go before the face of the Lord to prepare his ways;

77 To give knowledge of <u>salvation unto his people by the remission of their sins</u>, 78 <u>Through the tender mercy of our God</u>; whereby the dayspring from on high hath visited us,

79 <u>To give light to them that sit in dark-ness</u> and in the shadow of death, <u>to guide our feet into the way of peace</u>.

John grew in the nurture and admonition of the Lord. Verse 80:

80 And the child grew, and waxed [grew] strong in spirit, and was in the deserts till the day of his shewing unto Israel.

4

Luke 2

The Roman Empire, like many governments today, called for a census of their citizens to be taxed. Luke 2:1-3:

> 1 **And it came to pass in those days, that there went out a decree from Caesar Augustus, that all the world should be taxed.**
>
> 2 **(And this taxing was first made when Cyrenius was governor of Syria.) 3 And all went to be taxed, every one into his own city.**

In order to monitor the payment of taxes, the citizens were required to appear in person. Verses 4-5:

> 4 **And Joseph also went up from Gali-**

lee, out of the city of Nazareth, into Judaea, unto the city of David, which is
called Bethlehem; (because he was of
the house and lineage of David:)

5 To be taxed with Mary his espoused
wife, being great with child.

The time for the birth of Jesus came while they
were in Bethlehem. The beloved story of His birth is
recorded by Luke. Verses 6-7:

6 And so it was, that, while they were
there, the days were accomplished that
she should be delivered.

7 And she brought forth her firstborn
son, and wrapped him in swaddling
clothes, and laid him in a manger; because there was no room for them in the
inn.

The name Bethlehem is comprised of two
words which are "Beth" meaning "house of" and "le-
hem" which means "bread." So, the Savior Who
would be called the Bread of Life was born in Davids
city. The surrounding countryside had shepherds
tending their sheep. Verses 8-9:

8 And there were in the same country shepherds abiding in the field, keeping watch over their flock by night.

9 And, lo, the angel of the Lord came upon them, and the glory of the Lord shone round about them: and they were sore afraid.

The word "angel" simply means "messenger." God uses them to deliver His messages.. Let us look at a prophecy from the Prophet Isaiah. It tells of Jesus' purpose and future destiny. Isaiah 9:6-8:

6 For unto us a child is born, unto us a son is given: and [1] the government shall be upon his shoulder: and his name shall be called Wonderful, Counsellor, The mighty God, The everlasting Father, The Prince of Peace.

7 Of [2] <u>the increase of his government and peace there shall be no end</u>, [3] <u>upon the throne of David, and upon his kingdom</u>, to order it, and to establish it with judgment and with justice from henceforth even <u>for ever</u>. The zeal of the LORD of hosts will perform this.

8 The Lord sent a word into Jacob, and it hath lighted upon Israel.

God is sending light to those who are in darkness. Notice the numbering I placed within the text above. This announcement confirms that Jesus, the Son of David, will become the eternal King Who, as promised, will rule from David's throne forever.

The following is the message delivered to the shepherds. Luke 2:10-12:

10 And the angel said unto them, Fear not: for, behold, I bring you good tidings of great joy, which shall be to all people.

11 <u>For unto you is born this day in the city of David a Saviour, which is Christ the Lord.</u>

12 And this shall be a sign unto you; Ye shall find the babe wrapped in swaddling clothes, lying in a manger.

The host of heaven could not contain their jubilance and broke forth with praises. Verses 13-14:

13 And suddenly there was with the an-

gel a multitude of the heavenly host praising God, and saying,

14 Glory to God in the highest, and <u>on earth peace, good will toward men</u>.

This was no judgment. It was God proclaiming peace and good will to all men!

The shepherds were told by the angel how they could find this child. They hurried to see this site in Bethlehem. Verses 15-16:

15 And it came to pass, as the angels were gone away from them into heaven, the shepherds said one to another, Let us now go even unto Bethlehem, and see this thing which is come to pass, which the Lord hath made known unto us.

16 And they came with haste, and found Mary, and Joseph, and the babe lying in a manger.

After witnessing this scene, they departed and brought the wonderful news of the angelic announcement and the birth of the Child — the Promised Messiah. Verses 17-18:

17 And when they had seen it, they made known abroad the saying which was told them concerning this child.

18 And all they that heard it wondered at those things which were told them by the shepherds.

Everything that happened, Mary watched and wondered. Verse 19:

19 But Mary kept all these things, and pondered them in her heart.

The shepherds returned to their posts tending their sheep. They too remember the events of that night. Verse 20:

20 And the shepherds returned, glorifying and praising God for all the things that they had heard and seen, as it was told unto them.

Jesus was born a son of Abraham and was subject to the Mosaic Law. Everything required of Him would be done according to the Law of Moses. Verse 21:

21 And when eight days were accomplished for the circumcising of the child, his name was called JESUS, which was so named of the angel before he was conceived in the womb.

The Mosaic Law requires women who give birth to wait a period of forty day called "her purification." After that, she is free to travel. Every child is a gift from God. Every male born into the house of Israel must be presented or officially introduced to the Lord. Verses 22-23:

22 And when the days of her purification according to the law of Moses were accomplished, they brought him to Jerusalem, to present him to the Lord;

23 (As it is written in the law of the Lord, Every male that openeth the womb shall be called holy to the Lord;)

And, the required sacrifice was made. Verse 24:

24 And to offer a sacrifice according to that which is said in the law of the Lord, A pair of turtledoves, or two young pigeons.

While the parents were with Jesus at the Temple, there was a certain man named Simeon. He was waiting to see the "consolation of Israel." The word "consolation" means "comforting or alleviating misery; refreshing the mind or spirit." Simeon was waiting to see the arrival of the promised Messiah, the Son of David — the hope of Israel. Verses 25-27:

> **25 And, behold, there was a man in Jerusalem, whose name was Simeon; and the same man was just and devout, waiting for the consolation of Israel: and the Holy Ghost was upon him.**
>
> **26 And it was revealed unto him by the Holy Ghost, that he should not see death, before he had seen the Lord's Christ [Anointed].**
>
> **27 And he came by the Spirit into the temple: and when the parents brought in the child Jesus, to do for him after the custom of the law,**

Simeon had now seen the Hope of Israel! He was comforted and could rest with his ancestors. Verses 28-35:

> **28 Then took he him up in his arms, and blessed God, and said, 29 Lord, now lettest thou thy servant depart in peace,**

according to thy word: 30 For mine eyes have seen thy salvation, 31 Which thou hast prepared before the face of all people; 32 A light to lighten the Gentiles, and the glory of thy people Israel.

33 And Joseph and his mother marvelled at those things which were spoken of [about] him.

34 And Simeon blessed them, and said unto Mary his mother, Behold, this child is set for the fall and rising again of many in Israel; and for a sign which shall be spoken against;

35 (Yea, a sword shall pierce through thy own soul also,) that the thoughts of many hearts may be revealed.

Simeon had spoken by prophetic word foretelling the future of Israel. Jesus would be the cause of polarization in Israel: those for Him and those against Him.

Anna was an elderly woman who prayed and fasted at the Temple day and night. Verses 36-39:

36 And there was one Anna, a prophet-

ess, the daughter of Phanuel, of the tribe of Aser: she was of a great age, and had lived with an husband seven years from her virginity;

37 And <u>she</u> was a widow of about fourscore and four years, which departed not from the temple, but <u>served God with fastings and prayers night and day</u>.

38 And she coming in that instant gave thanks likewise unto the Lord, and spake of him to all them that looked for <u>redemption in Jerusalem</u>.

39 And when they had performed all things according to the law of the Lord, they returned into Galilee, to their own city Nazareth.

Having fulfilled all that was required by the Law, Mary, Joseph, and the Child returned to Nazareth.

Very little is written about Jesus' early years. The Bible does not tell us what we want to know. It tells us what God wants us to know. Jesus' early years were not integral to His mission. Verse 40:

40 And the child grew, and waxed [grew] strong in spirit, filled with wisdom: and the grace of God was upon him.

One other event is recorded. It would have been about the time of His Bar Mitzvah. In Hebrew, it means "son of the commandment" or Mosaic Law. Jesus may have been in Jerusalem for preparation for that event. Verses 41-45:

41 Now his parents went to Jerusalem every year at the feast of the passover.

42 And when he was twelve years old, they went up to Jerusalem after the custom of the feast. 43 And when they had fulfilled the days, as they returned, the child Jesus tarried behind in Jerusalem; and Joseph and his mother knew not of it.

44 But they, supposing him to have been in the company, went a day's journey; and they sought him among their kinsfolk and acquaintance. 45 And when they found him not, they turned back again to Jerusalem, seeking him.

Can you imagine the parents' anguish? They

were distraught. They frantically looked for the Child entrusted to them by God. Verses 46-48:

> 46 And it came to pass, that <u>after three days they found him in the temple</u>, sitting in the midst of the doctors, both hearing them, and asking them questions. 47 And all that heard him were astonished at his understanding and answers.

> 48 And when they [his parents] saw him, they were amazed: and his mother said unto him, Son, why hast thou thus dealt with us? behold, thy father and I have sought thee sorrowing.

They found Him in the Temple with the Pharisees who are doctors of the Law. Notice His response to His parents. Verses 49-50:

> 49 And he said unto them, How is it that ye sought me? wist [knew] ye not that I must be about my Father's business? 50 And they understood not the saying which he spake unto them.

This time Jesus went with His parents as they returned to their hometown of Nazareth. Verse 51:

51 And he went down with them, and came to Nazareth, and was subject [obedient] unto them: but his mother kept all these sayings in her heart.

This following sentence is the final remark concerning the Jesus' life prior to His ministry. Verse 52:

52 And Jesus increased in wisdom and stature, and in favour with God and man.

5

Luke 3

Luke's narrative moves to John the Baptist whose ministry announces the arrival of "the Lamb of God." The following allows us to date this period of time. There are various calculations made to arrive at a date. I use Daniel's timeline which he received from God to estimate the date to be 27 AD. Explained in both *Letters To Theophilus* and *The Glorious Destiny of Israel* we arrive at the date of the crucifixion of 30 AD. His earthly ministry with His Twelve was three years. As a confirmation, forty years following His being "cut off," Jerusalem was destroyed by the Romans in 70 AD. Luke 3:1-2:

> 1 **Now in the fifteenth year of the reign of Tiberius Caesar, Pontius Pilate being governor of Judaea, and Herod being tetrarch of Galilee, and his brother Philip tetrarch of Ituraea and of the region of**

Trachonitis, and Lysanias the tetrarch of Abilene,

2 Annas and Caiaphas being the high priests, the word of God came unto John [the Baptist] the son of Zacharias in the wilderness.

God sent John the Baptist to call the people to repentance. This is a turning away from sin and turning back to Him. As a symbol of that life-changing event, he would baptize the penitent with water. John was a Jew, born to Jewish parents, and called by God to call the people of Israel to repent. Notice, that if they repented, then they would receive "remission" of sins; and not "forgiveness" of sins. Verse 3:

3 And he came into all the country about Jordan, preaching <u>the baptism of repentance for the remission of sins</u>;

John is the one who would precede the Messiah's Coming. He was foretold by Isaiah. Verses 4-6:

4 As it is written in the book of the words of Esaias the prophet, saying, The voice of one crying in the wilderness, Prepare ye the way of the Lord, make his paths straight.

5 Every valley shall be filled, and every mountain and hill shall be brought low; and the crooked shall be made straight, and the rough ways shall be made smooth;

6 <u>And all flesh shall see the salvation of God</u>.

Jesus walked among both Jews and Gentiles. He was seen by all men. However, He came to fulfill or confirm the promises made to the fathers. (See Romans 15:8.)

It is the children of Israel who are the ones that John the Baptist called to repentance. He spoke to the Jews who came out into the desert to see and hear him preach. Verses 7-8:

7 Then said he [John] to the multitude that came forth to be baptized of him, O generation of vipers, who hath warned you to flee from the wrath to come?

8 Bring forth therefore fruits worthy of repentance, and begin not to say within yourselves, We have Abraham to [as] our father: for I say unto you, That God is able of these stones to raise up children unto Abraham.

In the Gospel of Luke, the theme remains the same. True repentance is evidenced by fruits of repentance showing the change in a person's life. From John's ministry, through Jesus' teaching, and, later, in the Hebrew epistles, good works are to demonstrate sincere faith. The Apostle James provides us with proof. The message to those who follow the Gospel of the Kingdom is unchanged. James 2:20-22:

> 20 **But wilt thou know, O vain man, that faith without works is dead?** 21 <u>**Was not Abraham our father justified by works, when he had offered Isaac his son upon the altar?**</u>

> 22 <u>**Seest thou how faith wrought with his works, and by works was faith made perfect?**</u>

John the Baptist refers to the imminent judgment. Luke 3:9:

> 9 **And now also the axe is laid unto the root of the trees: every tree therefore which bringeth not forth good fruit is hewn down, and cast into the fire.**

Those Jews who listened to him asked a question. Verses 10-11:

> 10 **And the people asked him, saying, What shall we do then?**
>
> 11 **He answereth and saith unto them, He that hath two coats, let him impart to him that hath none; and he that hath meat, let him do likewise.**

Charity shown towards others is one way to show faith through actions or works.

A "publican" is "someone who acts on behalf of the Roman government to collect tax revenue from the public." They were not liked by the people. Verses 12-14:

> 12 **Then came also publicans to be baptized, and said unto him, Master, what shall we do? 13 And he said unto them, Exact no more than that which is appointed you.**
>
> 14 **And the soldiers likewise demanded of him, saying, And what shall we do? And he said unto them, Do violence to no man, neither accuse any falsely; and**

be content with your wages.

Like the two faithful that Mary and Joseph met at the Temple, many Jews earnestly waited for the promised Messiah. All those who surrounded John the Baptist wondered if he were not the Messiah. Verse 15:

15 **And as the people were in expectation, and all men mused in their hearts of [about] John, whether he were the Christ, or not;**

John answers them by comparing himself with the coming Messiah. Verses 16-18:

16 **John answered, saying unto them all, I indeed baptize you with water; but one mightier than I cometh, the latchet of whose shoes I am not worthy to unloose: he shall baptize you with the Holy Ghost and with fire:**

17 **Whose fan is in his hand, and he will throughly purge his floor, and will gather the wheat into his garner [granary]; but the chaff he will burn with fire unquenchable.**

18 And many other things in his exhortation preached he unto the people.

During his ministry, John publicly condemned King Herod for his inappropriate relationship with his brother's wife. As a result, Herod had John imprisoned. Verses 19-20:

19 But Herod the tetrarch, being reproved by him [John] for Herodias his brother Philip's wife, and for all the evils which Herod had done, **20** Added yet this above all, that he shut up John in prison.

Like all the others who came to John to be baptized, Jesus came to fulfill all righteousness. Verses 21-22:

21 Now when all the people were baptized, it came to pass, that Jesus also being baptized, and praying, the heaven was opened,

22 And the Holy Ghost descended in a bodily shape like a dove upon him, and a voice came from heaven, which said, <u>Thou art my beloved Son; in thee I am well pleased.</u>

The Gospel of Matthew records Jesus' geneaology beginning with Abraham and King David. Matthew's purpose was to establish the legitimacy of Jesus' right to David's throne. Jesus is also the promised Seed of Abraham. Luke records His geneaology beginning with Joseph and follows it back to Adam. His purpose was to establish Jesus as the Son of Man. Paul explains the significance of this in 1 Corinthians 15:21-22:

> **21 For since by man came death, by man came also the resurrection of the dead.**
>
> **22 For as in Adam all die, even so in Christ shall all be made alive.**

Let us put it another way. The first Man was Adam. His original sin caused all men to be under the curse. Then, God sent Jesus, the Son of Man, as the second Adam. Jesus would fulfill God's requirements for all Mankind. Through this second Adam, all will be made alive again. However, do not confuse this with universal salvation. That is certainly not the case. The Apostle John quotes Jesus in John 5:28-29:

> **28 Marvel not at this: for the hour is coming, in the which <u>all [ALL] that are in the graves shall hear his voice</u>,**

29 And [ALL] shall come forth; <u>they that have done good, unto the resurrection of life; and they that have done evil, unto the resurrection of damnation</u>.

Luke provides the geneaology of Jesus Christ beginning with Joseph, Jesus' surrogate father, and ending with Adam. Luke 3:23-38:

23 And Jesus himself began to be about thirty years of age, being (as was supposed) the son of Joseph, which was the son of Heli, **24** Which was the son of Matthat, which was the son of Levi, which was the son of Melchi, which was the son of Janna, which was the son of Joseph,

25 Which was the son of Mattathias, which was the son of Amos, which was the son of Naum, which was the son of Esli, which was the son of Nagge, **26** Which was the son of Maath, which was the son of Mattathias, which was the son of Semei, which was the son of Joseph, which was the son of Juda,

27 Which was the son of Joanna, which was the son of Rhesa, which was the son

of Zorobabel, which was the son of
Salathiel, which was the son of Neri, 28
Which was the son of Melchi, which
was the son of Addi, which was the son
of Cosam, which was the son of
Elmodam, which was the son of Er,

29 Which was the son of Jose, which was
the son of Eliezer, which was the son of
Jorim, which was the son of Matthat,
which was the son of Levi, 30 Which was
the son of Simeon, which was the son of
Juda, which was the son of Joseph,
which was the son of Jonan, which was
the son of Eliakim,

31 Which was the son of Melea, which
was the son of Menan, which was the
son of Mattatha, which was the son of
Nathan, which was the son of David, 32
Which was the son of Jesse, which was
the son of Obed, which was the son of
Booz, which was the son of Salmon,
which was the son of Naasson,

33 Which was the son of Aminadab,
which was the son of Aram, which was
the son of Esrom, which was the son of
Phares, which was the son of Juda,

34 Which was the son of Jacob, which was the son of Isaac, which was the son of Abraham, which was the son of Thara, which was the son of Nachor,

35 Which was the son of Saruch, which was the son of Ragau, which was the son of Phalec, which was the son of Heber, which was the son of Sala, 36 Which was the son of Cainan, which was the son of Arphaxad, which was the son of Sem, which was the son of Noe, which was the son of Lamech,

37 Which was the son of Mathusala, which was the son of Enoch, which was the son of Jared, which was the son of Maleleel, which was the son of Cainan, 38 Which was the son of Enos, which was the son of Seth, which was the son of Adam, which was the son of God.

6

Luke 4

After Jesus' baptism, the Holy Spirit led Him into the wilderness to be tested. Israel was led by Moses into the Wilderness. There, God would test their faith. Would they listen to God? Would they believe Him? It did not go well for them. Due to their lack of faith, they were left to wander in the Wilderness: not for forty days, but for forty years.

Jesus was led out into the Wilderness alone. Likewise, He would also be tested. Luke 4:1-2:

> 1 And Jesus being full of the Holy Ghost returned from Jordan, and was led by the Spirit into the wilderness,

> 2 Being forty days tempted of [by] the devil. And in those days he did eat nothing: and when they were ended, he

afterward hungered.

Believers can easily be led astray for one reason. They are not sure about what God said. Think of Satan twisting what God said to Adam and Eve. Jesus was tested by Satan three times. Each time, Jesus responds by using the Word of God. Verses 3-13:

Test #1:

> 3 **And the devil said unto him, If thou be the Son of God, command this stone that it be made bread.**
>
> 4 **And Jesus answered him, saying, <u>It is written</u>, That man shall not live by bread alone, but by every word of God.**

Test #2:

> 5 **And the devil, taking him up into an high mountain, shewed unto him all the kingdoms of the world in a moment of time. 6 And the devil said unto him, All this power will I give thee, and the glory of them: for that is delivered unto me; and to whomsoever I will I give it. 7 If thou therefore wilt worship me, all shall be thine.**

8 And Jesus answered and said unto him, Get thee behind me, Satan: for <u>it is written</u>, Thou shalt worship the Lord thy God, and him only shalt thou serve.

Test #3:

9 And he brought him to Jerusalem, and set him on a pinnacle of the temple, and said unto him, If thou be the Son of God, cast thyself down from hence: 10 For it is written, He shall give his angels charge over thee, to keep thee: 11 And in their hands they shall bear thee up, lest at any time thou dash thy foot against a stone.

12 And Jesus answering said unto him, <u>It is said</u>, Thou shalt not tempt [test] the Lord thy God. 13 And when the devil had ended all the temptation, he departed from him for a season.

Jesus was able to withstand the tests or temptations of Satan. How? Jesus depended upon the Word of God alone for against such truth nothing can prevail. Upon the successful conclusion of this testing, Jesus began His ministry. Verses 14-15:

14 And Jesus returned in the power of the Spirit into Galilee: and there went out a fame of him through all the region round about. **15** And he taught in their synagogues, being glorified of [by] all.

His first stop was at the synagogue in His hometown of Nazareth. Often, members of the synagogue, were invited to the bema to read from the Scripture. Verses 16-19:

16 And he came to Nazareth, where he had been brought up: and, as his custom was, he went into the synagogue on the sabbath day, and stood up for to read.

17 And there was delivered unto him the book of the prophet Esaias. And when he had opened the book, he found the place where it was written,

18 The Spirit of the Lord is upon me, because <u>he hath anointed me to preach the gospel to the poor; he hath sent me to heal the brokenhearted, to preach deliverance to the captives, and recovering of sight to the blind, to set at liberty them that are bruised,</u> **19** <u>To preach the acceptable year of the Lord.</u>

At this point, Jesus closes the scroll, gives it to the attendant, and returns to His seat. All eyes in the congregation were on Him. Why? We will see in a moment. Verse 20:

20 And he closed the book, and he gave it again to the minister, and sat down. And the eyes of all them that were in the synagogue were fastened on him.

Now, He makes a proclamation to the people. Verse 21:

21 And he began to say unto them, <u>This day is this scripture fulfilled in your ears</u>.

Let us stop for a moment and consider the significance of His proclamation. We need to look at the text which Jesus read. The issue here has to do with the word "and." This word can sometimes be a time-signal. The best way to explain this is by an example. Richard was born in London and died in Boston. These points happened consecutively, but they could not have happened concurrently. These two events happened in the order stated, but they did not happen at the same time. There was a lapse in time between them. Such is the case with the following Scripture. We will divide it where the time lapse happens. Here is the first portion which Jesus read. Isaiah 61:1-2a:

> 1 **The Spirit of the Lord GOD is upon me; because the LORD hath anointed me to preach good tidings unto the meek; he hath sent me to bind up the brokenhearted, to proclaim liberty to the captives, and the opening of the prison to them that are bound;**
>
> 2 **To proclaim the acceptable year of the LORD, . . .**

This is the portion of the Scripture which Jesus proclaimed was fulfilled within their hearing.

All eyes were on Him because they knew the Scripture and He stopped in the middle! You see the later part of that Scripture, following the "and," would not happen until the Judgment. Verse 2b:

> 2 **. . . and the day of vengeance of our God; to comfort all that mourn;**

The day of God's vengeance or retribution will come. However, while Jesus is present on the earth, He will "preach the gospel to the poor . . . heal the brokenhearted . . . preach deliverance to the captives, and recovering of sight to the blind . . . set at liberty them that are bruised . . . [and] preach the acceptable year of the Lord" (v. 18-19).

Many present knew Jesus and His family for He had grown up there. Luke 4:22-30:

> 22 And all bare him witness, and wondered at the gracious words which proceeded out of his mouth. And they said, Is not this Joseph's son?

> 23 And he said unto them, Ye will surely say unto me this proverb, Physician, heal thyself: whatsoever we have heard done in Capernaum, do also here in thy country.

> 24 And he said, Verily I say unto you, No prophet is accepted in his own country. 25 But I tell you of a truth, many widows were in Israel in the days of Elias, when the heaven was shut up three years and six months, when great famine was throughout all the land;

> 26 But unto none of them was Elias sent, save unto Sarepta, a city of Sidon, unto a woman that was a widow. 27 And

> many lepers were in Israel in the time of Eliseus the prophet; and none of them was cleansed, saving Naaman the Syrian.
>
> 28 And all they in the synagogue, when they heard these things, were filled with wrath [indignation],
>
> 29 And rose up, and thrust him out of the city, and led him unto the brow of the hill whereon their city was built, that they might cast him down headlong. 30 But he passing through the midst of them went his way,

Jesus was rejected in His Own synagogue by those who knew Him. He so angered them that they would have taken Him to the top of the hill and thrown Him down head first. But, with the brush of His hand, he walk right through the middle of them.

Jesus went on His way and entered the city of Capernaum on the northern part of the Sea of Galilee. Verses 31-34:

> 31 And came down to Capernaum, a city of Galilee, and taught them on the sabbath days. 32 And they were astonished

54

at his doctrine: for his word was with power.

33 And in the synagogue there was a man, which had a spirit of an unclean devil [demon], and cried out with a loud voice, 34 Saying, Let us alone; what have we to do with thee, thou Jesus of Nazareth? art thou come to destroy us? I know thee who thou art; the Holy One of God.

Most of us are not used to encountering unclean spirits or demons. However, it was a common occurrence in this time. Paul states in his letter to the Ephesians, "For we wrestle not against flesh and blood, but against principalities, against powers, against the rulers of the darkness of this world, against spiritual wickedness in high places" (Eph. 6:12). The opposition was well aware of Who Jesus was and what was going to happen to them in the coming Judgment. Verse 35:

35 And Jesus rebuked him, saying, Hold thy peace, and come out of him. And when the devil [demon] had thrown him in the midst, he came out of him, and hurt him not.

Jesus commands and the unclean spirits obey. His reputation spread throughout the region. This brought many people who were curious about Who He was and what He could do for them. Verses 36-37:

> 36 And they were all amazed, and spake among themselves, saying, What a word is this! for with authority and power he commandeth the unclean spirits, and they come out.

> 37 And the fame of him went out into every place of the country round about.

Jesus departed from where He was teaching and went to Peter's home. Verses 38-39:

> 38 And he arose out of the synagogue, and entered into Simon's house. And Simon's wife's mother was taken with a great fever; and they besought him for her.

> 39 And he stood over her, and rebuked the fever; and it left her: and immediately she arose and ministered unto them.

By evening, a crowd had gathered outside Peter's home. People from far and wide brought to Jesus all those who were sick. Verses 40-41:

> 40 **Now when the sun was setting, all they that had any sick with divers [various] diseases brought them unto him; and he laid his hands on every one of them, and healed them.**

> 41 **And devils also came out of many, crying out, and saying, <u>Thou art Christ the Son of God</u>. And he rebuking them suffered [allowed] them not to speak: for they knew that he was Christ.**

The next morning, Jesus left for a secluded place, but the people found Him. In the following, Jesus refers to His gospel message for the first time. It is the "good news" of the Kingdom. Verses 42-44:

> 42 **And when it was day, he departed and went into a desert place: and the people sought him, and came unto him, and stayed him, that he should not depart from them.**

> 43 **And he said unto them, <u>I must preach the kingdom of God</u> to other cities also:**

for therefore [that reason] am I sent.

44 And he preached in the synagogues of Galilee.

7

Luke 5

The Lake of Gennesaret is another name for the Sea of Galilee. Jesus stood along its shore and called to two fishermen. Luke 5:1-3:

1 And it came to pass, that, as the people pressed upon him to hear the word of God, he stood by the lake of Gennesaret, 2 And saw two ships standing by the lake: but the fishermen were gone out of them, and were washing their nets.

3 And he entered into one of the ships, which was Simon's, and prayed [asked] him that he would thrust out a little from the land. And he sat down, and taught the people out of the ship.

This allowed Jesus some distance between Himself and the crowd so that He could teach them. Verses 4-11:

4 Now when he had left [finished] speaking, he said unto Simon, Launch out into the deep, and let down your nets for a draught [sweep for fish].

5 And Simon answering said unto him, Master, we have toiled all the night, and have taken nothing: nevertheless at thy word I will let down the net. 6 And when they had this done, they inclosed a great multitude of fishes: and their net brake.

7 And they beckoned unto their partners, which were in the other ship, that they should come and help them. And they came, and filled both the ships, so that they began to sink.

8 When Simon Peter saw it, he fell down at Jesus' knees, saying, Depart from me; for I am a sinful man, O Lord. 9 For he was astonished, and all that were with him, at the draught of the fishes which they had taken:

10 And so was also James, and John, the sons of Zebedee, which were partners with Simon. And Jesus said unto Simon, Fear not; from henceforth thou shalt catch men. **11** And when they had brought their ships to land, they forsook all, and followed him.

Jesus and the men He chose to follow Him arrived in another city. There was a man who had leprosy which was a disease much feared. Verses 12-14:

12 And it came to pass, when he was in a certain city, behold a man full of leprosy: who seeing Jesus fell on his face, and besought him, saying, Lord, if thou wilt, thou canst make me clean.

13 And he [Jesus] put forth his hand, and touched him, saying, I will: be thou clean. And immediately the leprosy departed from him. **14** And he charged [instructed] him to tell no man: but go, and shew thyself to the priest, and offer for thy cleansing, according as Moses commanded, for a testimony unto them.

Instead, the man who was overjoyed by his healing shared the news with everyone. This increased the size of the crowds who sought after Him. Verse 15:

> **15 But so much the more went there a fame abroad of him: and great multitudes came together to hear, and to be healed by him of their infirmities.**

As Jesus' ministry continued, He regularly talk to His Father through prayer. Verse 16:

> **16 And he withdrew himself into the wilderness, and prayed.**

Prayer is connecting with God the Father. When Jesus returned to the people, He was greeted by the religious leaders who had heard about Him. They came to observe. Verses 17-20:

> **17 And it came to pass on a certain day, as he was teaching, that there were Pharisees and doctors of the law sitting by, which were come out of every town of Galilee, and Judaea, and Jerusalem: and the power of the Lord was present to heal them.**

> **18 And, behold, men brought in a bed a man which was taken with a palsy: and they sought means to bring him in, and**

to lay him before him.

19 And when they could not find by what way they might bring him in because of the multitude, they went upon the housetop, and let [lowered] him down through the tiling with his couch into the midst before Jesus.

20 And when he saw their faith, he said unto him, Man, thy sins are forgiven thee.

As they listened, the scribes and Pharisees heard what they believed to be blasphemy. Only God can forgive sins! They found Jesus' words highly offensive. Verses 21-26:

21 And the scribes and the Pharisees began to reason, saying, Who is this which speaketh blasphemies? Who can forgive sins, but God alone?

22 But when Jesus perceived their thoughts, he answering said unto them, What reason ye in your hearts? 23 Whether is easier, to say, Thy sins be forgiven thee; or to say, Rise up and walk?

24 But that ye may know that the Son of man hath power upon earth to forgive sins, (he said unto the sick of the palsy,) I say unto thee, Arise, and take up thy couch, and go into thine house.

25 And immediately he rose up before them, and took up that whereon he lay, and departed to his own house, glorifying God.

26 And they were all amazed, and they glorified God, and were filled with fear, saying, We have seen strange things to day.

They traveled on and, along the way, they met a man named Levi who was a publican or tax collector. He was also known as Matthew, the writer of the Gospel of Matthew. Verses 27-29:

27 And after these things he went forth, and saw a publican, named Levi, sitting at the receipt of custom: and he said unto him, Follow me.

28 And he left all, rose up, and followed him. 29 And Levi made him a great feast in his own house: and there was a great

company of publicans and of others that sat down with them.

As a tax collector, Matthew was a wealthy man and not much liked by the people. In his home he hosted a dinner with other publicans and Jesus attended.

The religious leaders of Israel were on a different social plane. They would not mix with those of dubious character. Knowing their thoughts, Jesus addresses their objections. Verses 30-32:

30 But their scribes and Pharisees murmured against his disciples, saying, Why do ye eat and drink with publicans and sinners?

31 And Jesus answering said unto them, They that are whole need not a physician; but they that are sick. 32 I came not to call the righteous, but sinners to repentance.

They asked Jesus a question comparing the disciples of John the Baptist with His Own. Verses 33-35:

33 And they said unto him, Why do the disciples of John fast often, and make prayers, and likewise the disciples of

the Pharisees; but thine eat and drink?

34 And he said unto them, Can ye make the children of the bridechamber fast, while the bridegroom is with them? 35 But the days will come, when the bridegroom shall be taken away from them, and then shall they fast in those days.

Have you ever wondered why Jesus chose to go to the people of Israel and not their religious leaders. To change a government, would we not go to its leaders? Jesus teaches with a parable which answers this question. Verses 36-39:

36 And he spake also a parable unto them; No man putteth a piece of a new garment upon an old; if otherwise, then both the new maketh a rent, and the piece that was taken out of the new agreeth not with the old.

37 And no man putteth new wine into old bottles; else the new wine will burst the bottles, and be spilled, and the bottles shall perish.

38 But new wine must be put into new bottles; and both are preserved.

39 No man also having drunk old wine straightway desireth new: for he [the man] saith, The old is better.

It is a fact to which I personally attest. Most people do not want to change. This especially applies to those of the old guard who guard against change. They hold to their customs, traditions, and teachings of the men who taught them. Those in leadership rarely want to change. Jesus was teaching something different. His teaching is like new wine. It must be put in new bottles which represent the common people and not the religious leaders.

8

Luke 6

It was the day of rest following a full week of ministry. They were under constant surveillance by Israel's religious leaders. In their view, this upstart was going to be a problem for their established religion. Luke 6:1-2:

> **1 And it came to pass on the second sabbath after the first, that he went through the corn fields; and his disciples plucked the ears of corn, and did eat, rubbing them in their hands.**
>
> **2 And certain of the Pharisees said unto them, Why do ye that which is not lawful to do on the sabbath days?**

The Law requires that the sabbath be kept separate and honored above the others days.

Jesus responds to them with something they should have already known. Verses 3-5:

> 3 And Jesus answering them said, Have ye not read so much as this, what David did, when himself was an hungred, and they which were with him;
>
> 4 How he went into the house of God, and did take and eat the shewbread, and gave also to them that were with him; which it is not lawful to eat but for the priests alone?
>
> 5 And he said unto them, That <u>the Son of man</u> is Lord also of the sabbath.

Another week passed and Jesus was teaching in another synagogue. Verses 6-7:

> 6 And it came to pass also on another sabbath, that he entered into the synagogue and taught: and there was a man whose right hand was withered.
>
> 7 And the scribes and Pharisees watched him, [to see] whether he would heal on the sabbath day; that they might find an accusation against him.

Knowing their thoughts, Jesus decided to teach them concerning this man. Verse 8:

> 8 **But he knew their thoughts, and said to the man which had the withered hand, Rise up, and stand forth in the midst. And he arose and stood forth.**

With all the people in attendance looking at this man, He asks the religious leaders a question. Verse 9:

> 9 **Then said Jesus unto them, I will ask you one thing; Is it lawful on the sabbath days to do good, or to do evil? to save life, or to destroy it?**

I picture Jesus waiting for the question to be considered by the leaders and the people there. Then, He healed the man. Verses 10-11:

> 10 **And looking round about upon them all, he said unto the man, Stretch forth thy hand. And he did so: and his hand was restored whole as the other.**

> 11 **And they were filled with madness; and communed one with another what they might do to Jesus.**

Again, Jesus sought solitude with the Father praying all night. In the morning, He calls His Twelve to Him. Verses 12-13:

> 12 **And it came to pass in those days, that he went out into a mountain to pray, and continued all night in prayer to God.**
>
> 13 **And when it was day, he called unto him his disciples: and of them he chose twelve, whom also he named apostles;**

In Matthew 10:2-5, we find a list of the Twelve whom He called to be His Apostles. Luke provides us with a list also. Verses 14-16:

> 14 **Simon, (whom he also named Peter,) and Andrew his brother, James and John, Philip and Bartholomew, 15 Matthew and Thomas, James the son of Alphaeus, and Simon called Zelotes,**
>
> 16 **And Judas the brother of James, and Judas Iscariot, which also was the traitor.**

If you make a comparison of these two lists, then you will see that Judas, the brother of James, was also called Thaddaeus or Lebbaeus. This differentiates him from the Judas who betrayed Him.

People came to see Jesus from as far away as Tyre and Sidon, both located on the coast of the Mediterranean Sea. Verses 17-19:

> 17 **And he came down with them, and stood in the plain, and the company of his disciples, and a great multitude of people out of all Judaea and Jerusalem, and from the sea coast of Tyre and Sidon, which came to hear him, and to be healed of their diseases;**
>
> 18 **And they that were vexed with unclean spirits: and they were healed.** 19 **And the whole multitude sought to touch him: for there went virtue out of him, and healed them all.**

Can you imagine this crowd and each person wanting to touch Him?

Here, Jesus teaches His disciples what many call the Beatitudes. They are blessings upon those who keep them and woes upon those who do not. Verses 20-38:

20 And he lifted up his eyes on his disciples, and said, Blessed be ye poor: for yours is the kingdom of God.

21 Blessed are ye that hunger now: for ye shall be filled. Blessed are ye that weep now: for ye shall laugh.

22 Blessed are ye, when men shall hate you, and when they shall separate you from their company, and shall reproach you, and cast out your name as evil, for the Son of man's sake. 23 Rejoice ye in that day, and leap for joy: for, behold, your reward is great in heaven: for in the like manner did their fathers unto the prophets.

24 But woe unto you that are rich! for ye have received your consolation. 25 Woe unto you that are full! for ye shall hunger. Woe unto you that laugh now! for ye shall mourn and weep. 26 Woe unto you, when all men shall speak well of you! for so did their fathers to the false prophets.

27 But I say unto you which hear, Love your enemies, do good to them which

hate you, 28 Bless them that curse you, and pray for them which despitefully use you.

29 And unto him that smiteth [strikes] thee on the one cheek offer also the other; and him that taketh away thy cloke forbid not to take thy coat also.

30 Give to every man that asketh of thee; and of him that taketh away thy goods ask them not again. 31 And as ye would that men should do to you, do ye also to them likewise.

32 For if ye love them which love you, what thank have ye? for sinners also love those that love them. 33 And if ye do good to them which do good to you, what thank have ye? for sinners also do even the same. 34 And if ye lend to them of whom ye hope to receive, what thank have ye? for sinners also lend to sinners, to receive as much again.

35 But love ye your enemies, and do good, and lend, hoping for nothing again [in return]; and your reward shall be great, and ye shall be the children of

the Highest: for he is kind unto the un-
thankful and to the evil.

36 Be ye therefore merciful, as your Father also is merciful. 37 Judge not, and
ye shall not be judged: condemn not,
and ye shall not be condemned: forgive,
and ye shall be forgiven:

38 Give, and it shall be given unto you;
good measure, pressed down, and
shaken together, and running over,
shall men give into your bosom. For
with the same measure that ye mete
withal it shall be measured to you
again.

Jesus teaches the people with parables. These
stories are designed to explain spiritual truth using
familiar concepts. This has to do with them judging
each other for something they themselves do. Verses
39-45:

39 And he spake a parable unto them,
Can the blind lead the blind? shall they
not both fall into the ditch?

40 The disciple is not above his master:
but every one that is perfect shall be as

his master. 41 And why beholdest thou the mote that is in thy brother's eye, but perceivest [knows] not the beam that is in thine own eye?

42 Either how canst thou say to thy brother, Brother, let me pull out the mote that is in thine eye, when thou thyself beholdest not the beam that is in thine own eye? Thou hypocrite, cast out first the beam out of thine own eye, and then shalt thou see clearly to pull out the mote that is in thy brother's eye.

43 For a good tree bringeth not forth corrupt fruit; neither doth a corrupt tree bring forth good fruit. 44 For every tree is known by his own fruit. For of thorns men do not gather figs, nor of a bramble bush gather they grapes.

45 A good man out of the good treasure of his heart bringeth forth that which is good; and an evil man out of the evil treasure of his heart bringeth forth that which is evil: for of the abundance of the heart his mouth speaketh.

Jesus continues by questioning those who lis-

ten to Him. They call Him Lord, but do not do what
He says. Verses 46-49:

46 **And why call ye me, Lord, Lord, and
do not the things which I say?**

47 **Whosoever cometh to me, and heareth
my sayings, and doeth them, I will shew
you to whom he is like:**

48 **He is like a man which built an house,
and digged deep, and laid the foundation on a rock: and when the flood
arose, the stream beat vehemently upon
that house, and could not shake it: for it
was founded upon a rock.**

49 **But he that heareth, and doeth not, is
like a man that without a foundation
built an house upon the earth; against
which the stream did beat vehemently,
and immediately it fell; and the ruin of
that house was great.**

9

Luke 7

Jesus was outside Capernaum. This allowed for large crowds without raising suspicion by the Roman military. The people would come, sit, and listen to Him teach. Luke 7:1-10:

1 **Now when he had ended all his sayings in the audience of the people, he entered into Capernaum.**

2 **And a certain centurion's servant, who was dear unto him, was sick, and ready to die.** 3 **And when he heard of Jesus, he sent unto him the elders of the Jews, beseeching him that he would come and heal his servant.**

4 **And when they came to Jesus, they besought [urged] him instantly, saying,**

That he was worthy for whom he should do this: 5 For he loveth our nation, and he hath built us a synagogue.

6 Then Jesus went with them. And when he was now not far from the house, the centurion sent friends to him, saying unto him, Lord, trouble not thyself: for I am not worthy that thou shouldest enter under my roof:

7 Wherefore neither thought I myself worthy to come unto thee: but say in a word, and my servant shall be healed. 8 For I also am a man set under authority, having under me soldiers, and I say unto one, Go, and he goeth; and to another, Come, and he cometh; and to my servant, Do this, and he doeth it.

9 When Jesus heard these things, he marvelled at him, and turned him about, and said unto the people that followed him, I say unto you, I have not found so great faith, no, not in Israel. 10 And they that were sent, returning to the house, found the servant whole that had been sick.

Jesus would stay in an area and do miracles and healings because Jews require a sign from God to credential a prophet. After He had taught in an area, He would move onto another. Verses 11-12:

> 11 **And it came to pass the day after, that he went into a city called Nain; and many of his disciples went with him, and much people.**

> 12 **Now when he came nigh [near] to the gate of the city, behold, there was a dead man carried out, the only son of his mother, and she was a widow: and much people of the city was with her.**

The word "bier" refers to "a wooden frame used to carry a dead body to its burial." Verses 13-15:

> 13 **And when the Lord saw her, he had compassion on her, and said unto her, Weep not. 14 And he came and touched the bier: and they that bare him stood still. And he said, Young man, I say unto thee, Arise.**

> 15 **And he that was dead sat up, and began to speak. And he delivered him to his mother.**

The Jewish bury their dead as soon as possible after death, preferably on the same day. There can be no question as to the validity of the death since they were on their way to lay his body to rest. We can only imagine the shock of the crowd and the joy of the widow whose son was restored to her. Verses 16-17:

> 16 **And there came a fear on all: and they glorified God, saying, That a great prophet is risen up among us; and, That God hath visited his people.**

> 17 **And this rumour of him went forth throughout all Judaea, and throughout all the region round about.**

John the Baptist had disciples or students whom he taught and assisted him in his ministry. John sent his disciples to ask Jesus a question. Verses 18-23:

> 18 **And the disciples of John shewed [informed] him of all these things.**

> 19 **And John calling [sent] unto him two of his disciples sent them to Jesus, saying, Art thou he that should come? or look we for another?**

20 When the men were come unto him, they said, John Baptist hath sent us unto thee, saying, Art thou he that should come? or look we for another?

21 And in that same hour he cured many of their infirmities and plagues, and of evil spirits; and unto many that were blind he gave sight.

22 Then Jesus answering said unto them, Go your way, and tell John what things ye have seen and heard; how that the blind see, the lame walk, the lepers are cleansed, the deaf hear, the dead are raised, to the poor the gospel is preached.

23 And blessed is he, whosoever shall not be offended in [by] me.

John's disciples returned to him with Jesus' response. Jesus takes this opportunity to ask the people about John. Verses 24-28:

24 And when the messengers of John were departed, he began to speak unto the people concerning John, What went ye out into the wilderness for to see? A

reed shaken with the wind? 25 But what went ye out for to see? A man clothed in soft raiment? Behold, they which are gorgeously apparelled, and live delicately, are in kings' courts.

26 But what went ye out for to see? A prophet? Yea, I say unto you, and much more than a prophet.

27 This is he, of whom it is written, Behold, I send my messenger before thy face, which shall prepare thy way before thee. 28 For I say unto you, Among those that are born of women there is not a greater prophet than John the Baptist: but he that is least in the kingdom of God is greater than he.

The people believed John the Baptist was sent from God and chose to be baptized by him. However, the religious had rejected his baptism. Verses 29-30:

29 And all the people that heard him, and the publicans, justified God, being baptized with the baptism of John. 30 But the Pharisees and lawyers rejected the counsel of God against themselves,

being not baptized of him.

Jesus would rebuke the men who were the religious leaders of Israel. They were the blind leading the blind. The children of Abraham were spiritually lost. At the sending out of the Twelve, Jesus makes clear who the good news of the Kingdom is specifically intended for the lost sheep of the house of Israel. "But go rather to the lost sheep of the house of Israel. And as ye go, preach, saying, the kingdom of heaven is at hand" (Matt. 10:6-7).

Jesus compares the current generation to children. When teaching, there are those who are on milk and cannot be fed meat which is more advanced. Verses 31-35:

> 31 **And the Lord said, Whereunto then shall I liken [compare] the men of this generation? and to what are they like? 32 They are like unto children sitting in the marketplace, and calling one to another, and saying, We have piped unto you, and ye have not danced; we have mourned to you, and ye have not wept.**
>
> 33 **For John the Baptist came neither eating bread nor drinking wine; and ye say, He hath a devil. 34 The Son of man**

is come eating and drinking; and ye say, Behold a gluttonous man, and a wine-bibber, a friend of publicans and sinners! 35 But wisdom is justified of [by] all her children.

During the meal, a woman came to Jesus and did something unusual. Verses 36-38:

36 And one of the Pharisees desired him that he would eat with him. And he went into the Pharisee's house, and sat down to meat [a meal].

37 And, behold, a woman in the city, which was a sinner, when she knew that Jesus sat at meat in the Pharisee's house, brought an alabaster box of ointment,

38 And stood at his feet behind him weeping, and began to wash his feet with tears, and did wipe them with the hairs of her head, and kissed his feet, and anointed them with the ointment.

The Pharisee knew this woman and, let us just say, that she was a sinner. He thought to himself that Jesus has no idea who is touching Him. Verse 39:

39 Now when the Pharisee which had bidden him saw it, he spake within himself, saying, This man, if he were a prophet, would have known who and what manner of woman this is that toucheth him: for she is a sinner.

Jesus knew his thoughts and answered him. Verses 40-50:

40 And Jesus answering said unto him, Simon, I have somewhat to say unto thee. And he saith, Master, say on.

41 There was a certain creditor which had two debtors: the one owed five hundred pence, and the other fifty. 42 And when they had nothing to pay, he frankly forgave them both. Tell me therefore, which of them will love him most?

43 Simon answered and said, I suppose that he, to whom he forgave most. And he said unto him, Thou hast rightly judged.

44 And he turned to the woman, and said unto Simon, Seest thou this woman? I

entered into thine house, thou gavest me no water for my feet: but she hath washed my feet with tears, and wiped them with the hairs of her head.

45 Thou gavest me no kiss: but this woman since the time I came in hath not ceased to kiss my feet.

46 My head with oil thou didst not anoint: but this woman hath anointed my feet with ointment.

47 Wherefore I say unto thee, Her sins, which are many, are forgiven; for she loved much: but to whom little is forgiven, the same loveth little.

48 <u>And he said unto her, Thy sins are forgiven</u>. 49 And they that sat at meat with him began to say within themselves, Who is this that forgiveth sins also?

50 And he said to the woman, <u>Thy faith hath saved thee; go in peace.</u>

10

Luke 8

Jesus followed the same approach with each city He visited and there were many. He took with Him the Twelve teaching them as they went. One woman is known by many who have read the gospel accounts. She is Mary Magdalene who had been saved by Jesus from possession by seven demons. Luke 8:1-3:

> 1 And it came to pass afterward, that he went throughout every city and village, preaching and shewing the glad tidings of the kingdom of God: and the twelve were with him,
>
> 2 And certain women, which had been healed of evil spirits and infirmities, Mary called Magdalene, out of whom went seven devils,

3 And Joanna the wife of Chuza Herod's steward, and Susanna, and many others, which ministered unto him [Herod] of their substance [for their livelihood].

These women were from Herod's household and others came to hear Jesus speak. They listened as He told the parable of the sower and the seed. Verses 4-8:

4 And when much people were gathered together, and were come to him out of every city, he spake by a parable:

5 A sower went out to sow his seed: and as he sowed, some fell by the way side; and it was trodden down, and the fowls of the air devoured it.

6 And some fell upon a rock; and as soon as it was sprung up, it withered away, because it lacked moisture.

7 And some fell among thorns; and the thorns sprang up with it, and choked it.

8 And other fell on good ground, and sprang up, and bare fruit an hundredfold. And when he had said these

things, he cried [out], He that hath ears
to hear, let him hear.

Jesus used parables but the meaning was often
not understood by the people. Later, when His
Twelve came to Him privately, He would explain its
meaning. Verses 9-15:

9 And his disciples asked him, saying,
What might this parable be? 10 And he
said, Unto you it is given to know the
mysteries of <u>the kingdom of God</u>: but to
others in parables; that seeing they
might not see, and hearing they might
not understand.

11 Now the parable is this: The seed is
the word of God.

12 Those by the way side are they that
hear; then cometh the devil, and taketh
away the word out of their hearts, lest
they should believe and be saved.

13 They on the rock are they, which,
when they hear, receive the word with
joy; and these have no root, which for a
while believe, and in time of temptation
fall away.

14 And that which fell among thorns are they, which, when they have heard, go forth, and are choked with cares and riches and pleasures of this life, and bring no fruit to perfection.

15 But that on the good ground are they, which in an honest and good heart, having heard the word, keep it, and bring forth fruit with patience.

Jesus told another parable about a lit candle. Its light represents knowledge of the gospel or truth. Those to whom the light is given must use it and not hide it. Verses 16-18:

16 No man, when he hath lighted a candle, covereth it with a vessel, or putteth it under a bed; but setteth it on a candlestick, that they which enter in may see the light.

17 For nothing is secret, that shall not be made manifest [known]; neither any thing hid, that shall not be known and come abroad.

18 Take heed therefore how ye hear: for whosoever hath, to him shall be given;

and whosoever hath not, from him shall be taken even that which he seemeth to have.

Mary, Jesus' mother, came with His brethren to see Him. However, because of the crowd, they were unable to reach Him. They sent a message to Him that they were there. Verses 19-21:

19 **Then came to him his mother and his brethren, and could not come at him for the press [crowd].**

20 **And it was told him by certain which said, Thy mother and thy brethren stand without, desiring to see thee.**

21 **And he answered and said unto them, My mother and my brethren are these which hear the word of God, and do it.**

His response gives us an insight into His present ministry. He was no longer Jesus from Nazareth, the Son of Mary. He was the Messiah of Israel and the Son of God. The children of Israel who hear and do what the word of God requires are now His family.

The following situation tests the faith of the Twelve. It shows that they did not yet fully understand Who Jesus is. Verses 22-25:

> 22 Now it came to pass on a certain day, that he went into a ship with his disciples: and he said unto them, Let us go over unto the other side of the lake. And they launched forth.

> 23 But as they sailed he fell asleep: and there came down a storm of wind on the lake; and they were filled with water, and were in jeopardy. 24 And they came to him, and awoke him, saying, Master, master, we perish. Then he arose, and rebuked the wind and the raging of the water: and they ceased, and there was a calm.

> 25 <u>And he said unto them, Where is your faith?</u> And they being afraid wondered, saying one to another, What manner of man is this! for he commandeth even the winds and water, and they obey him.

Much of Jesus' early ministry took place around the Sea of Galilee for two reason. First, the water provided a means of transportation away from the crowds. Second, the religious leaders in Jerusalem would be a threat to His ministry. Therefore, He remained a distance from there until the last portion of His ministry. Jesus is arriving at a region called the Gadarenes which is located not far from the southeastern shore of the Sea of Galilee. Verses 26-28:

> 26 **And they arrived at the country of the Gadarenes, which is over against Galilee. 27 And when he went forth to land, there met him out of the city a certain man, which had devils [demons] long time, and ware no clothes, neither abode in any house, but in the tombs.**
>
> 28 **When he saw Jesus, he cried out, and fell down before him, and with a loud voice said, <u>What have I to do with thee, Jesus, thou Son of God most high?</u> I beseech thee, torment me not.**

Many of the children of Israel did not know Jesus and the Twelve would eventually learn. However, the unclean spirit in the realm of darkness immediately recognized Jesus is the Son of God!

Jesus commands these spirits to be silent. They knew that their appointed time had not yet come so they ask Him what He wants from them. We are told there is a nearby herd of pigs. Verses 29-33:

29 (For he had commanded the unclean spirit to come out of the man. For oftentimes it had caught him: and he was kept bound with chains and in fetters; and he brake the bands, and was driven of [by] the devil into the wilderness.)

30 And Jesus asked him, saying, What is thy name? And he said, Legion: because many devils were entered into him.

31 And they besought him that he would not command them to go out into the deep. 32 And there was there an herd of many swine feeding on the mountain: and they besought him that he would suffer them to enter into them. And he suffered [allowed] them.

33 Then went the devils out of the man, and entered into the swine: and the herd ran violently down a steep place into the lake, and were choked.

The demons asked Jesus to cast them out from this man into that herd and He did as they requested. There were those who tended to the pigs and they watched as they ran off the cliff and were drown. Verse 34:

34 **When they that fed them saw what was done, they fled, and went and told it in the city and in the country.**

The possessed man was now in his right mind and sitting with Jesus. All those from the area knew this man. Now, he was changed. Verses 35-36:

35 **Then they went out to see what was done; and came to Jesus, and found the man, out of whom the devils were departed, sitting at the feet of Jesus, clothed, and in his right mind: and they were afraid.**

36 **They also which saw it told them by what means he that was possessed of the devils was healed.**

The response from the community was one of fear not fully understanding what had happened. As a result, they begged Jesus to leave them and He did. Verse 37:

37 **Then the whole multitude of the country of the Gadarenes round about besought [begged] him to depart from them; for they were taken with great fear: and he went up into the ship, and**

returned back again.

What happened to the man who was healed? He desired to stay with Jesus, but was directed to return to his home. He would be a testimony to others of Jesus' healing. Verses 38-39:

> 38 **Now the man out of whom the devils were departed besought [begged] him that he might be [remain] with him: but Jesus sent him away, saying,**

> 39 **Return to thine own house, and shew how great things God hath done unto thee. And he went his way, and published [made known] throughout the whole city how great things Jesus had done unto him.**

Jesus returned to Capernaum where He was known. Verse 40:

> 40 **And it came to pass, that, when Jesus was returned, the people gladly received him: for they were all waiting for him.**

A man named Jairus who was a ruler in the synagogue in Capernaum heard He had returned. He came to Jesus concerning his daughter. Verses 41-42:

41 And, behold, there came a man named Jairus, and he was a ruler of the synagogue: and he fell down at Jesus' feet, and besought him that he would come into his house:

42 For he had one only daughter, about twelve years of age, and she lay a dying. But as he [Jesus] went the people thronged him.

A woman with a bleeding disorder came to Jesus on His way to Jairus' house. Verses 43-48:

43 And a woman having an issue of blood twelve years, which had spent all her living upon physicians, neither could be healed of [by] any,

44 [She] Came behind him, and touched the border of his garment: and immediately her issue of blood stanched.

45 And Jesus said, Who touched me? When all denied, Peter and they that were with him said, Master, the multitude throng thee and press thee, and

sayest thou, Who touched me? 46 And Jesus said, Somebody hath touched me: for I perceive that virtue is gone out of me.

47 And when the woman saw that she was not hid, she came trembling, and falling down before him, she declared unto him before all the people for what cause she had touched him, and how she was healed immediately.

48 And he said unto her, Daughter, be of good comfort: <u>thy faith hath made thee whole; go in peace.</u>

While Jesus was delayed in reaching Jairus' house, there came a messenger who brought news. His daughter had died. Verses 49-56:

49 While he yet spake, there cometh one from the ruler of the synagogue's house, saying to him, Thy daughter is dead; trouble not the Master.

50 But when Jesus heard it, he answered him, saying, Fear not: believe only, and she shall be made whole. 51 And when he came into the house, he suffered

100

[allowed] no man to go in, save [except] Peter, and James, and John, and the father and the mother of the maiden.

52 And all wept, and bewailed her: but he said, Weep not; she is not dead, but sleepeth. 53 And they laughed him to scorn, knowing that she was dead.

54 And he put them all out, and took her by the hand, and called, saying, Maid, arise. 55 And her spirit came again, and she arose straightway: and he commanded to give her meat [something to eat].

56 And her parents were astonished: but he charged them that they should tell no man what was done.

11

Luke 9

With sufficient training of the Twelve complete, Jesus sends them out to preach the Gospel of the Kingdom. He gives them instructions they are to follow. Luke 9:1-5:

1 Then he called his twelve disciples together, and gave them power and authority over all devils, and to cure diseases. 2 And he sent them to preach the kingdom of God, and to heal the sick.

3 And he said unto them, Take nothing for your journey, neither staves, nor scrip, neither bread, neither money; neither have two coats apiece.

4 And whatsoever house ye enter into, there abide, and thence depart. 5 And

whosoever will not receive you, when ye go out of that city, shake off the very dust from your feet for a testimony against them.

As instructed, they preached the gospel and healed the sick. Verse 6:

6 **And they departed, and went through the towns, preaching the gospel, and healing every where.**

As the Twelve expanded Jesus' work, Herod was confused and thought that John the Baptist had risen from the grave. Was it Elijah or another of the prophets of old that had risen again? Herod was the one who had John the Baptist killed. Verses 7-9:

7 **Now Herod the tetrarch heard of all that was done by him: and he was perplexed, because that it was said of some, that John was risen from the dead;**

8 **And of some, that Elias had appeared; and of others, that one of the old prophets was risen again.**

9 **And Herod said, John have I beheaded: but who is this, of whom I hear**

such things? And he desired to see him.

These Apostles would be the ones who would carry on His work when He was no longer with them. Receiving their reports, He took them to a place where He could teach them privately. Verse 10:

10 **And the apostles, when they were re-turned, told him all that they had done. And he took them, and went aside pri-vately into a desert place belonging to the city called Bethsaida.**

It was not long and the crowds found them again. Verses 11-12:

11 **And the people, when they knew it, followed him: and he received them, and spake unto them of the kingdom of God, and healed them that had need of healing.**

12 **And when the day began to wear away, then came the twelve, and said unto him, Send the multitude away, that they may go into the towns and country round about, and lodge, and get victuals [food]: for we are here in a de-sert[ed] place.**

The crowd had stayed with Jesus most of the day and evening was coming. Since it was a remote place, the Twelve suggested that Jesus send them away so they could buy some food. Instead, He surprises them and tells them to feed the crowd. Verses 13-17:

> **13 But he said unto them, Give ye them to eat. And they said, We have no more but [than] five loaves and two fishes; except we should go and buy meat for all this people.**

> **14 For they were about five thousand men. And he said to his disciples, Make them sit down by fifties in a company [group]. 15 And they did so, and made them all sit down.**

> **16 Then he [Jesus] took the five loaves and the two fishes, and looking up to heaven, he blessed them, and brake, and gave to the disciples to set before the multitude.**

> **17 And they did eat, and were all filled: and there was taken up of fragments that remained to them twelve baskets.**

106

Luke tells us that there were about five thousand men, but this did not include women and children.

When Jesus was alone with His disciples, He asked them who did the people believe Him to be. Verses 18-22:

18 **And it came to pass, as he was alone praying, his disciples were with him: and he asked them, saying, Whom say the people that I am?**

19 **They answering said, John the Baptist; but some say, Elias; and others say, that one of the old prophets is risen again.**

20 **He said unto them, But whom say ye that I am? Peter answering said, <u>The Christ [Anointred One] of God</u>.**

21 **And he [Jesus] straitly charged them, and commanded them to tell no man that thing; 22 Saying, <u>The Son of man must suffer many things, and be rejected of the elders and chief priests and scribes, and be slain, and be raised the third day</u>.**

Jesus teaches them about the sacrifices that they will need to make. They will need to separate themselves from the cares of the world and follow only after Him. Verses 23-27:

23 And he said to them all, If any man will come after me, let him deny himself, and take up his cross daily, and follow me. 24 For whosoever will save his life shall lose it: but whosoever will lose his life for my sake, the same shall save it.

25 For what is a man advantaged, if he gain the whole world, and lose himself, or be cast away?

26 For whosoever shall be ashamed of me and of my words, of him shall the Son of man be ashamed, when he shall come in his own glory, and in his Father's, and of the holy angels.

27 But I tell you of a truth, there be some standing here, which shall not taste of death, till they see the kingdom of God.

He was referring to the few who would soon witness the Transfiguration.

About a week later, Jesus took Peter, James, and John. Together they went up a mountain to pray. It was during this time that they witnessed Jesus being changed in His appearance. Verses 28-29:

> 28 **And it came to pass about an eight days after these sayings, he took Peter and John and James, and went up into a mountain to pray.**

> 29 **And as he prayed, the fashion of his countenance was altered, and his raiment [clothes] was white and glistering.**

There appeared two other men who were talking with Jesus. They talked together about His coming death. Verses 30-31:

> 30 **And, behold, there talked with him two men, which were Moses and Elias:**
> 31 **Who appeared in glory, and spake of his decease [death] which he should accomplish at Jerusalem.**

The three whom Jesus brought with Him were witnesses to this glorious event. Jesus was invested with power by God to act as Israel's King as He committed Himself to the task that lay before Him.

The three men were weary and may have fallen asleep. When they woke up they saw Jesus and the two men standing together. Verse 32:

> 32 But Peter and they that were with him were heavy with sleep: and when they were awake, they saw his glory, and the two men that stood with him.

A "tabernacle" is a "temporary habitation" which is often portable. As Moses and Elijah were leaving, Peter offered to build them each a tabernacle. This may have been to encourage His visitors to stay longer. Verse 33:

> 33 And it came to pass, as they departed from him, Peter said unto Jesus, Master, it is good for us to be here: and let us make three tabernacles; one for thee, and one for Moses, and one for Elias: not knowing what he said.

A cloud came and surrounded them. Verses 34-36:

> 34 While he thus spake, there came a cloud, and overshadowed them: and they feared as they entered into the cloud.

110

35 And there came a voice out of the cloud, saying, <u>This is my beloved Son: hear him</u>.

36 And when the voice was past, Jesus was found alone. And they kept it close, and told no man in those days any of those things which they had seen.

As they were returning from the mountain, a crowd of people greeted Him. Verses 37-42:

37 And it came to pass, that on the next day, when they were come down from the hill, much people met him. 38 And, behold, a man of the company cried out, saying, Master, I beseech thee, look upon my son: for he is mine only child.

39 And, lo, a spirit taketh him, and he suddenly crieth out; and it teareth him that he foameth again, and bruising him hardly departeth from him. 40 And I besought [begged] thy disciples to cast him out; and they could not.

41 And Jesus answering said, O faithless and perverse generation, how long shall I be with you, and suffer you? Bring thy

son hither [here].

42 And as he was yet a coming, the devil [demon] threw him down, and tare him. And Jesus rebuked the unclean spirit, and healed the child, and delivered him again to his father.

The people that witnessed the miracle were astonished and talked among themselves. Verse 43:

43 And they were all amazed at the mighty power of God. But while they wondered every one at all things which Jesus did, he said unto his disciples,

Jesus had only a short time left with His disciples. He desired for them to know what would happen to Him. Yet, they did not understand. Verses 44-45:

44 Let these sayings sink down into your ears: for the Son of man shall be delivered into the hands of men.

45 But they understood not this saying, and it was hid from them, that they perceived it not: and they feared to ask him of [about] that saying.

The Twelve were not immune to the ways of the world. As they argued among themselves, Jesus asked what is it they are discussing. Verses 46-48:

46 Then there arose a reasoning among them, which of them should be greatest.

47 And Jesus, perceiving the thought of their heart, took a child, and set him by him,

48 And said unto them, Whosoever shall receive this child in my name receiveth me: and whosoever shall receive me receiveth him that sent me: for he that is least among you all, the same shall be great.

There was a man who was casting out demons in the name of Jesus, but he was not part of their company. The disciples ask Jesus if he should be stopped. Verses 49-50:

49 And John answered and said, Master, we saw one casting out devils in thy name; and we forbad him, because he followeth not with us.

50 And Jesus said unto him, Forbid him

not: for he that is not against us is for us.

Knowing the fierce opposition, Jesus responds by saying that those who are not against them are for them.

During Jesus' ministry, He had avoided going to Jerusalem until the end. This was because of the religious leaders of Israel. Verses 51-55:

> 51 **And it came to pass, when the time was come that he should be received up, he stedfastly set his face [was determined] to go to Jerusalem,**
>
> 52 **And sent messengers before his face: and they went, and entered into a village of the Samaritans, to make ready for him. 53 And they did not receive him, because his face was as though he would go to Jerusalem.**
>
> 54 **And when his disciples James and John saw this, they said, Lord, wilt thou that we command fire to come down from heaven, and consume them, even as Elias did? 55 But he turned, and rebuked them, and said, Ye know not what manner of spirit ye are of.**

His disciples expected a confrontation. The Hebrew Scripture speaks about a coming judgment. However, this judgment will come at the end of the Tribulation. Do you remember Jesus reading from Isaiah in His synagogue? Isaiah 61:1-2a:

> **1 The Spirit of the Lord GOD is upon me; because the LORD hath anointed me to preach good tidings unto the meek; he hath sent me to bind up the brokenhearted, to proclaim liberty to the captives, and the opening of the prison to them that are bound;**

> **2 To proclaim the acceptable year of the LORD, . . .**

His disciples were expecting something contrary to this. They asked if He would destroy His enemies? Here is His response. Luke 9:56:

> **56 For <u>the Son of man is not come to destroy</u> men's lives, <u>but to save</u> them. And they went to another village.**

As they continued traveling towards Jerusalem, one man came to them and pledged to go with Jesus wherever He would go. Verses 57-58:

57 And it came to pass, that, as they went in the way, a certain man said unto him, Lord, I will follow thee whithersoever thou goest.

58 And Jesus said unto him, Foxes have holes, and birds of the air have nests; but the Son of man hath not where to lay his head.

Another comes desiring to follow Jesus, but he must first go and bury his father. Verses 59-60:

59 And he said unto another, Follow me. But he said, Lord, suffer [allow] me first to go and bury my father.

60 Jesus said unto him, Let the dead bury their dead: but go thou and preach the kingdom of God.

Finally, a third comes and, likewise, needed to say goodbye to friends and family. Verses 61-62:

61 And another also said, Lord, I will follow thee; but let me first go bid them farewell, which are at home at my house.

62 And Jesus said unto him, No man, having put his hand to the plough, and looking back, is fit for the kingdom of God.

12

Luke 10

After sending out the Twelve, Jesus chose another group of men to be sent out into the fields which were ready for the harvest. Luke 10:1-8:

1 After these things the Lord appointed other seventy also, and sent them two and two before his face into every city and place, whither [where] he himself would come.

2 Therefore said he unto them, The harvest truly is great, but the labourers are few: pray ye therefore the Lord of the harvest, that he would send forth labourers into his harvest.

3 Go your ways: behold, I send you forth as lambs among wolves. 4 Carry neither

purse, nor scrip, nor shoes: and salute no man by the way. 5 And into whatsoever house ye enter, first say, Peace be to this house.

6 And if the son of peace be there, your peace shall rest upon it: if not, it shall [re]turn to you again. 7 And in the same house remain, eating and drinking such things as they give: for the labourer is worthy of his hire. Go not from house to house.

8 And into whatsoever city ye enter, and they receive you, eat such things as are set before you:

They are to remain with one host and be grateful for whatever provisions are given to them. Verses 9-16:

9 And heal the sick that are therein, and say unto them, The kingdom of God is come nigh unto [near to] you.

10 But into whatsoever city ye enter, and they receive you not, go your ways out into the streets of the same, and say,

11 Even the very dust of your city, which cleaveth on us, we do wipe off against you: notwithstanding be ye sure of this, that the kingdom of God is come nigh [near] unto you.

12 But I say unto you, that it shall be more tolerable in that day for Sodom, than for that city.

13 Woe unto thee, Chorazin! woe unto thee, Bethsaida! for if the mighty works had been done in Tyre and Sidon, which have been done in you, they had a great while ago repented, sitting in sackcloth and ashes.

14 But it shall be more tolerable for Tyre and Sidon at the judgment, than for you. 15 And thou, Capernaum, which art exalted to heaven, shalt be thrust down to hell.

16 He that heareth you heareth me; and he that despiseth you despiseth me; and he that despiseth me despiseth him that sent me.

The Seventy returned to the Lord filled with

exuberance over their success. Jesus makes a comment about Satan and his downfall. Verses 17-18:

> 17 **And the seventy returned again with joy, saying, Lord, even the devils [demons] are subject unto us through thy name.**
>
> 18 **And he said unto them, I beheld Satan as lightning fall from heaven.**

In the above verse, Jesus refers to an event when Satan and his rebel angels are cast out of heaven. It is mentioned in Revelation 12:7-9:

> 7 **And there was war in heaven: Michael and his angels fought against the dragon; and the dragon fought and his angels,** 8 **And prevailed not; neither was their place found any more in heaven.**
>
> 9 <u>**And the great dragon was cast out, that old serpent, called the Devil, and Satan, which deceiveth the whole world: he was cast out into the earth, and his angels were cast out with him**</u>**.**

He continues speaking to the Seventy. Luke 10:19-20:

19 Behold, I give unto you power to tread on serpents and scorpions, and over all the power of the enemy: and nothing shall by any means hurt you.

20 Notwithstanding in this rejoice not, that the spirits are subject unto you; but rather rejoice, because your names are written in heaven.

Encouraged by the success of the Seventy, Jesus rejoices also. For it is God Who reveals Himself to people. Verses 21-22:

21 In that hour Jesus rejoiced in spirit, and said, I thank thee, O Father, Lord of heaven and earth, that thou hast hid these things from the wise and prudent, and hast revealed them unto babes: even so, Father; for so it seemed good in thy sight.

22 All things are delivered to me of [by] my Father: and no man knoweth who the Son is, but the Father; and who the Father is, but the Son, and he to whom the Son will reveal him.

Only the Father knows the Son. Only the Father is

known by the Son and those to whom the Son reveals Him.

When Jesus was alone with His disciples, He explains that not all who want to see will see. However, the disciples have seen what others could not. Verses 23-24:

> **23 And he turned him unto his disciples, and said privately, Blessed are the eyes which see the things that ye see:**

> **24 For I tell you, that many prophets and kings have desired to see those things which ye see, and have not seen them; and to hear those things which ye hear, and have not heard them.**

A lawyer stood up and asked Jesus a question. Verses 25-26:

> **25 And, behold, a certain lawyer stood up, and tempted [tested] him, saying, Master, what shall I do to inherit eternal life?**

> **26 He said unto him, What is written in the law? how readest thou?**

Jesus would sometimes teach by asking questions. Verses 27-37:

27 And he answering said, Thou shalt love the Lord thy God with all thy heart, and with all thy soul, and with all thy strength, and with all thy mind; and thy neighbour as thyself.

28 And he said unto him, Thou hast answered right: this do, and thou shalt live.

29 But he, willing to justify himself, said unto Jesus, And who is my neighbour?

30 And Jesus answering said, A certain man went down from Jerusalem to Jericho, and fell among thieves, which stripped him of his raiment, and wounded him, and departed, leaving him half dead.

31 And by chance there came down a certain priest that way: and when he saw him, he passed by on the other side.

32 And likewise a Levite, when he was at the place, came and looked on him, and passed by on the other side.

33 But a certain Samaritan, as he jour-
neyed, came where he was: and when
he saw him, he had compassion on him,
34 And went to him, and bound up his
wounds, pouring in oil and wine, and
set him on his own beast, and brought
him to an inn, and took care of him.

35 And on the morrow when he departed, he took out two pence, and gave
them to the host, and said unto him,
Take care of him; and whatsoever thou
spendest more, when I come again, I
will repay thee.

36 <u>Which now of these three, thinkest
thou, was [a] neighbour unto him that
fell among the thieves?</u>

37 And he said, He that shewed mercy
on him. Then said Jesus unto him, Go,
and do thou likewise.

Jesus and His disciples moved on to another
place where they would meet two sisters, Mary and
Martha. They were invited into their home. Verses
38-42:

38 Now it came to pass, as they went, that he entered into a certain village: and a certain woman named Martha received him into her house. 39 And she had a sister called Mary, which also sat at Jesus' feet, and heard his word.

40 But Martha was cumbered about much serving, and came to him, and said, Lord, dost thou not care that my sister hath left me to serve alone? bid her therefore that she help me.

41 And Jesus answered and said unto her, Martha, Martha, thou art careful [full of care] and troubled about many things:

42 But one thing is needful: and Mary hath chosen that good part, which shall not be taken away from her.

13

Luke 11

Time for a reminder as we continue with this chapter. The Messiah came to fulfill the promises God made to the fathers — the fathers of the children of Israel. I know that many contemporary teachers and believers will disagree, but let us stick to the Word of God alone. (See Romans 15:8.) Jesus was sent to the Jews. He chose twelve Jews to be His disciples. The message of the Gospel of the Kingdom was taken to the Jews only. (See Matthew 10:2-7.) In the following, Jesus is asked by His disciples to give them an example of a prayer that they could follow. Luke 11:1-3:

> 1 **And it came to pass, that, as he was praying in a certain place, when he ceased, one of his disciples said unto him, Lord, teach us to pray, as John also taught his disciples.**

2 And he said unto them, When ye pray, say, Our Father which art in heaven, Hallowed [holy] be thy name. Thy kingdom come. Thy will be done, as in heaven, so in earth.

3 Give us day by day <u>our daily bread</u>.

When the Israelites were in the Wilderness with Moses, God provided them with food and water in the desert. He did this on a daily basis and met their daily needs. This was to teach Israel to be dependent upon God for everything.

There is another version of this prayer recorded by Matthew who was an eyewitness. Luke's gospel comes from information collected from eyewitnesses. Jesus may have repeated this model at other times which explains the difference between the version most people memorized as children. Matthew 6:9-13:

9 After this manner therefore pray ye: Our Father which art in heaven, Hallowed be thy name. **10** Thy kingdom come. Thy will be done in earth, as it is in heaven.

11 <u>Give us this day our daily bread</u>.

12 And <u>forgive us our debts, as we forgive our debtors</u>. **13** And lead us not into temptation, but deliver us from evil: For thine is the kingdom, and the power, and the glory, for ever. Amen.

The Gospel of Matthew includes two verses after this prayer. Jesus explains that forgiveness of the petitioners is dependent upon their forgiveness of others. The Gospel of Grace and the Gospel of the Kingdom differ on this point. Verses 14-15:

14 For if ye forgive men their trespasses, your heavenly Father will also forgive you: **15** But if ye forgive not men their trespasses, neither will your Father forgive your trespasses.

Now, let us compare this to Luke 11:4:

4 And forgive us our sins; for we also forgive every one that is indebted to us. And lead us not into temptation; but deliver us from evil.

Jesus continues to teach about the relationship between a believer and God. Verses 5-10:

5 And he said unto them, Which of you

shall have a friend, and shall go unto him at midnight, and say unto him, Friend, lend me three loaves;

6 For a friend of mine in his journey is come to me, and I have nothing to set before him? 7 And he from within shall answer and say, Trouble me not: the door is now shut, and my children are with me in bed; I cannot rise and give thee.

8 I say unto you, Though he will not rise and give him, because he is his friend, yet because of his importunity he will rise and give him as many as he needeth.

9 And I say unto you, Ask, and it shall be given you; seek, and ye shall find; knock, and it shall be opened unto you.

10 For every one that asketh receiveth; and he that seeketh findeth; and to him that knocketh it shall be opened.

Jesus gives another example of a child's request to his earthly father. He compares it to the relationship between a believer and God the Father. Verses 11-13:

11 If a son shall ask bread of any of you that is a father, will he give him a stone? or if he ask a fish, will he for a fish give him a serpent? 12 Or if he shall ask an egg, will he offer him a scorpion?

13 If ye then, being evil, know how to give good gifts unto your children: how much more shall your heavenly Father give the Holy Spirit to them that ask him?

Luke records the healing that took place of a man who was "dumb" which means "unable to speak." Jesus healed him and a controversy arose over whose power was used to accomplish this miracle! Verses 14-20:

14 And he was casting out a devil [demon], and it was dumb. And it came to pass, when the devil was gone out, the dumb spake; and the people wondered.

15 But some of them said, He casteth out devils through Beelzebub the chief of the devils. 16 And others, tempting [tested] him, sought of him a sign from heaven.

17 But he, knowing their thoughts, said unto them, Every kingdom divided against itself is brought to desolation; and a house divided against a house falleth.

18 If Satan also be divided against himself, how shall his kingdom stand? because ye say that I cast out devils through Beelzebub.

19 And if I by Beelzebub cast out devils, by whom do your sons cast them out? therefore shall they be your judges.

20 But <u>if I with the finger of God cast out devils, no doubt the kingdom of God is come upon you.</u>

Jesus gives them a story about demons once they have left their host. Without filling the vacancy with God, that emptiness is soon filled. Verses 21-26:

21 When a strong man armed keepeth his palace, his goods are in peace:

22 But when a stronger than he shall come upon him, and overcome him, he taketh from him all his armour wherein

he trusted, and divideth his spoils.

23 He that is not with me is against me: and he that gathereth not with me scattereth.

24 When the unclean spirit is gone out of a man, he walketh through dry places, seeking rest; and finding none, he saith, I will return unto my house [from] whence I came out. 25 And when he cometh, he findeth it swept and garnished.

26 Then goeth he, and taketh to him seven other spirits more wicked than himself; and they enter in, and dwell there: and the last state of that man is worse than the first.

While Jesus was speaking a woman blessed the mother who bore and raised Him, but He instead blessed those who hear the Word of God and honor it by keeping it. Verses 27-28:

27 And it came to pass, as he spake these things, a certain woman of the company lifted up her voice, and said unto him, Blessed is the womb that bare thee, and

the paps [breasts from] which thou hast sucked.

28 But he said, Yea rather, <u>blessed are they that hear the word of God, and keep it</u>.

A large crowd had gathered to hear Him. For those who desired a sign, Jesus speaks of a sign to come. Do you recall the story of the Prophet Jonah who was swallowed by a great fish? Verse 29:

29 And when the people were gathered thick together, he began to say, This is an evil generation: they seek a sign; and there shall no sign be given it, but the sign of Jonas the prophet.

The prophet Jonah was in the belly of the great fish for three days. God sent him to the Gentile city of Nineveh. There, they listened and repented. Next, Jesus speaks about the Gentile Queen of Sheba. She came to test Solomon's wisdom by asking him difficult questions. When Solomon answered all of them, he left her amazed by his wisdom and the glory of his kingdom. She acknowledged that all Solomon possessed had come from the God of Israel. Knowledge of God's truth is light! Verses 30-36:

30 For as Jonas was a sign unto the Nine-vites, so shall also the Son of man be to this generation.

31 The queen of the south shall rise up in the judgment with the men of this generation, and condemn them: for she came from the utmost parts of the earth to hear the wisdom of Solomon; and, behold, a greater [One] than Solomon is here.

32 The men of Nineve [Nineveh] shall rise up in the judgment with this gener-ation, and shall condemn it: for they re-pented at the preaching of Jonas [Jo-nah]; and, behold, a greater [One] than Jonas is here.

33 No man, when he hath lighted a can-dle, putteth it in a secret place, neither under a bushel, but on a candlestick, that they which come in may see the light.

34 The light of the body is the eye: there-fore when thine eye is single, thy whole body also is full of light; but when thine eye is evil, thy body also is full of dark-

ness. 35 Take heed therefore that the light which is in thee be not darkness.

36 If thy whole body therefore be full of light, having no part dark, the whole shall be full of light, as when the bright shining of a candle doth give thee light.

The religious leaders remained focused on the Law, their customs, and traditions. Hearing Jesus, a Pharisee completely ignored what Jesus taught. Instead, he was amazed that Jesus did not ritually wash before eating. Even today, many people are blind to the truths of God because they focus on their religious customs, traditions, and vain philosophies or teachings of men. Verses 37-39:

37 And as he [Jesus] spake, a certain Pharisee besought him to dine with him: and he went in, and sat down to meat.

38 And when the Pharisee saw it, he marvelled that he had not first washed before dinner.

39 And the Lord said unto him, Now do ye Pharisees make clean the outside of the cup and the platter; but your inward

part is full of ravening and wickedness.

The word "fool" means "someone who is devoid of reason or the ability to understand." Verses 40-44:

40 Ye fools, did not he that made that which is without [outside] make that which is within [inside] also? 41 But rather give alms of such things as ye have; and, behold, all things are clean unto you.

42 But woe unto you, Pharisees! for ye tithe mint and rue [common garden herbs] and all manner of herbs, and pass over judgment and the love of God: these ought ye to have done, and not to leave the other undone.

43 Woe unto you, Pharisees! for ye love the uppermost seats in the synagogues, and greetings in the markets.

44 Woe unto you, scribes and Pharisees, hypocrites! for ye are as graves which appear not, and the men that walk over them are not aware of them.

Sensing Jesus' contempt against the religious

leaders, one of them confirms it. Verses 45-52:

45 Then answered one of the lawyers, and said unto him, Master, thus saying thou reproachest us also.

46 And he said, Woe unto you also, ye lawyers! for ye lade [load] men with burdens grievous to be borne [carried], and ye yourselves touch not the burdens with one of your fingers.

47 Woe unto you! for ye build the sepulchres of the prophets, and your fathers killed them. 48 Truly ye bear witness that ye allow the deeds of your fathers: for they indeed killed them, and ye build their sepulchres.

49 Therefore also said the wisdom of God, I will send them prophets and apostles, and some of them they shall slay and persecute: 50 That the blood of all the prophets, which was shed from the foundation of the world, may be required of this generation;

51 From the blood of Abel unto the blood of Zacharias, which perished be-

tween the altar and the temple: verily I say unto you, It shall be required of this generation.

52 Woe unto you, lawyers! for ye have taken away the key of knowledge: ye entered not in yourselves, and them that were entering in ye hindered.

These educated leaders were devoid of the truth. Yet, being empty of the truth themselves, they taught others as if they were superior in their knowledge. They desired that Jesus should speak more for the purpose of acquiring accusations against Him. Verses 53-54:

53 And as he said these things unto them, the scribes and the Pharisees began to urge him vehemently, and to provoke him to speak of many things:

54 Laying wait for him, and seeking to catch something out of his mouth, that [by which] they might accuse him.

14

Luke 12

The comments that Jesus made about the Pharisees goes far beyond ancient Israel's priests and scribes. It is far broader and applies to today's religious institutions. Men teach what they were taught by those who were taught by men who were taught. As they go, a little bit of their own thoughts and beliefs are added. In the following, Jesus calls this "leaven." This is the same as our present-day "yeast." It can double the size of bread by making it rise. Leaven is not limited to the past. Beware as the content in some sermons and lessons go far beyond the words in the Bible. Some churches that purport to "preach from the Bible" only use Scripture as a springboard for their own "philosophies of men."

Consider this. Say we transcribe a sermon and highlight in yellow the quotations of the Bible. What percentage of that sermon would be God's Word versus the words of man? Consider this commentary. The Word of God is printed in bold type to differentiate it between God's Word and my commentary. We go through the entire text verse by verse. As students of the Bible, we must test what is said. In a synagogue, Paul taught the Jews at Berea. Here is what is said about them. "These were more noble than those in Thessalonica, in that they received the word with all readiness of mind, and searched the scriptures daily, whether those things were so" (Acts 17:11). We are all called to be like the Bereans. Listen to what is being taught, but verify everything according to the Bible.

Jesus teaches His disciples in Luke 12:1-3:

1 In the mean time, when there were gathered together an innumerable multitude of people, insomuch that they trode [step upon] one upon another, he began to say unto his disciples first of all, <u>Beware ye of the leaven of the Pharisees, which is hypocrisy</u>.

2 For there is nothing covered, that shall not be revealed; neither hid, that shall not be known.

3 Therefore whatsoever ye have spoken

144

in darkness shall be heard in the light; and that which ye have spoken in the ear in closets shall be proclaimed upon the housetops.

The word "fear" when spoken about God often means "respect." Fearing God means having respect for what He says. Verses 4-5:

4 And I say unto you my friends, Be not afraid of them that kill the body, and after that have no more that they can do.

5 But I will forewarn you whom ye shall fear: Fear him, which after he hath killed hath power to cast into hell; yea, I say unto you, Fear him.

They should fear or respect God because He loves and cares about them. Verses 6-9:

6 Are not five sparrows sold for two farthings, and not one of them is forgotten before God?

7 But even the very hairs of your head are all numbered. Fear not therefore: ye are of more value than many sparrows.

8 Also I say unto you, Whosoever shall confess me before men, him shall the Son of man also confess before the angels of God: **9** But he that denieth me before men shall be denied before the angels of God.

Jesus warns about a sin that shall not be forgiven. First, Jesus is speaking to the lost sheep of the house of Israel. Second, He is speaking about the Gospel of the Kingdom. Do not get this confused with the Gospel of Grace taught by the Apostle Paul. Later, we find at the trial of Stephen, the first martyr, that he was filled with the Holy Spirit and was stoned. This was the offense that Jesus alluded to in the following. Verses 10-12:

10 And whosoever shall speak a word against the Son of man, it shall be forgiven him: but unto him that blasphemeth against the Holy Ghost it shall not be forgiven.

11 And when they bring you unto the synagogues, and unto magistrates, and powers, take ye no thought how or what thing ye shall answer, or what ye shall say:

146

12 For the Holy Ghost shall teach you in the same hour what ye ought to say.

Some who were there ask Him questions and He responds. Verses 13-15:

13 And one of the company said unto him, Master, speak to my brother, that he divide the inheritance with me.

14 And he said unto him, Man, who made me a judge or a divider over you? **15** And he said unto them, Take heed, and beware of covetousness: for a man's life consisteth not in the abundance of the things which he possesseth.

Jesus uses a parable to teach about earthly possessions. The Gospel of the Kingdom is about spiritual matters, therefore storing up treasure on earth is vanity or foolishness. Verses 16-21:

16 And he spake a parable unto them, saying, The ground of a certain rich man brought forth plentifully: **17** And he thought within himself, saying, What shall I do, because I have no room where to bestow [store] my fruits?

18 And he said, This will I do: I will pull down my barns, and build greater; and there will I bestow all my fruits and my goods. 19 And I will say to my soul, Soul, thou hast much goods laid up for many years; take thine ease, eat, drink, and be merry.

20 But God said unto him, Thou fool, this night thy soul [life] shall be required of thee: then whose shall those things be [belong], which thou hast provided? 21 So is he that layeth up treasure for himself, and is not rich toward God.

God has always wanted His people to depend on Him. In the Wilderness, He fed and provided water for both them and their livestock. In the frigid nights, He provided a pillar of fire for heat and in the oppressive heat He provided a cloud for shade. He still wants to provide for His people! However, His response is based upon their faith in Him. Verses 22-32:

22 And he said unto his disciples, Therefore I say unto you, Take no thought for your life, what ye shall eat; neither for the body, what ye shall put on.

23 The life is more than meat, and the body is more than raiment. 24 Consider the ravens: for they neither sow nor reap; which neither have storehouse nor barn; and God feedeth them: how much more are ye better than the fowls?

25 And which of you with taking thought [worry] can add to his stature one cubit? 26 If ye then be not able to do that thing which is least, why take ye thought for the rest [anything else]?

27 Consider the lilies how they grow: they toil not, they spin not; and yet I say unto you, that Solomon in all his glory was not arrayed like one of these.

28 If then God so clothe the grass, which is to day in the field, and to morrow is cast into the oven; how much more will he clothe you, O ye of little faith?

29 And seek not ye what ye shall eat, or what ye shall drink, neither be ye of doubtful mind. 30 For all these things do the nations of the world seek after: and your Father knoweth that ye have need of these things.

31 But [Instead] rather seek ye the kingdom of God; and all these things shall be added unto you.

32 <u>Fear not, little flock; for it is your Father's good pleasure to give you the kingdom.</u>

During Jesus' earthly ministry, the Kingdom was imminent and would be established in seven years—at the end of Jacob's Time of Trouble. For the Jews, this was wonderful news. The time clock from Daniel 9 was still running. The Gospel of the Kingdom was being preached. God will establish His eternal Kingdom. Jesus the Messiah will be crowned Israel's eternal King. Look at this prophecy. Jeremiah 30:4-9:

4 And these are the words that the LORD spake concerning Israel and concerning Judah. 5 For thus saith the LORD; We have heard a voice of trembling, of fear, and not of peace.

6 Ask ye now, and see whether a man doth travail with child? wherefore do I see every man with his hands on his loins, as a woman in travail, and all faces are turned into paleness?

7 Alas! for <u>that day is great</u>, so that none is like it: it is even <u>the time of Jacob's trouble</u>; <u>but he shall be saved out of it.</u>

8 For it shall come to pass in that day, saith the LORD of hosts, that I will break his yoke from off thy neck, and will burst thy bonds, and strangers shall no more serve themselves of him:

9 <u>But they shall serve the LORD their God, and David their king, whom I will raise up unto them.</u>

This is too important a subject to go into detail here. I recommend, for those interested in the Gospel of the Kingdom, reading *The Glorious Destiny of Israel: The Fulfillment of God's Promises and Prophecies to Israel.*

Believers who trust in God's providence and provision, could show their faith by selling their earthly treasures and giving the proceeds to the needy. Israel is a theocracy and the Commonwealth of Israel is to serve their eternal King. Luke 12:33-40:

33 Sell that [what] ye have, and give alms; provide yourselves bags which wax not old, a treasure in the heavens that faileth not, where no thief approacheth, neither moth corrupteth.

34 For where your treasure is, there will your heart be also.

35 Let your loins be girded about, and your lights burning; 36 And ye yourselves like unto men that wait for their lord, when he will return from the wedding; that when he cometh and knocketh, they may open unto him immediately.

37 Blessed are those servants, whom the lord when he cometh shall find watching: verily I say unto you, that he shall gird himself, and make them to sit down to meat [meal], and will come forth and serve them.

38 And if he shall come in the second watch, or come in the third watch, and find them so, blessed are those servants.

39 And this know, that if the goodman of the house had known what hour the thief would come, he would have watched, and not have suffered his

house to be broken through. 40 Be ye therefore ready also: for the Son of man cometh at an hour when ye think not.

Peter asks Jesus to whom is He speaking. Verses 41-48:

41 Then Peter said unto him, Lord, speakest thou this parable unto us, or even [is that to say] to all [everyone]?

42 And the Lord said, Who then is that faithful and wise steward, whom his lord shall make ruler over his household, to give them their portion of meat in due season?

43 Blessed is that servant, whom his lord when he cometh shall find so doing. 44 Of a truth I say unto you, that he will make him ruler over all that he hath.

45 But and if that servant say in his heart, My lord delayeth his coming; and shall begin to beat the menservants and maidens, and to eat and drink, and to be drunken;

46 The lord of that servant will come in

a day when he looketh not for him, and at an hour when he is not aware, and will cut him in sunder, and will appoint him his portion with the unbelievers.

47 And that servant, which knew his lord's will, and prepared not himself, neither did according to his will, shall be beaten with many stripes.

48 But he that knew not, and did commit things worthy of stripes, shall be beaten with few stripes. For unto whomsoever much is given, of him shall be much required: and to whom men have committed much, of him they will ask the more.

Some of what Jesus teaches has to do with His own future. What He has been given by God to accomplish, He is "straitened" or "committed" to accomplishing. The battle against good and evil continues and God has provided the solution in His Son. Verses 49-50:

49 I am come to send fire on the earth; and what will I, if it be already kindled [started]? 50 But I have a baptism to be baptized with; and how am I straitened till it be accomplished!

The baptism to which He refers is His Own baptism of physical death, burial, and resurrection. Verses 51-53:

> 51 **Suppose ye that I am come to give peace on earth? I tell you, Nay; but rather division: 52 For from henceforth there shall be five in one house divided, three against two, and two against three.**

> 53 **The father shall be divided against the son, and the son against the father; the mother against the daughter, and the daughter against the mother; the mother in law against her daughter in law, and the daughter in law against her mother in law.**

Some of Abraham's children will choose to believe God and the Gospel of the Kingdom. They are the remnant. Others, who are not his true children, will reject God and the Gospel of the Kingdom. They will even fight against those who do believe.

We are observant of natural things such as rain clouds. Seeing them in the distance, it signals the coming rain. Likewise, there are certain signs of the coming Kingdom. Verses 54-56:

54 And he said also to the people, When ye see a cloud rise out of the west, straightway ye say, There cometh a shower; and so it is.

55 And when ye see the south wind blow, ye say, There will be heat; and it cometh to pass.

56 Ye hypocrites, ye can discern the face of the sky and of the earth; but how is it that ye do not discern this time?

The people judge each other like adversaries and not as fellow members of the children of Abraham. Verse 57:

57 Yea, and why even of yourselves judge ye not what is right?

The chapter ends with words similar to those found in the Lord's Prayer. Matthew 6:11-12:

11 Give us this day our daily bread. **12** And forgive us our debts, as [in the same manner in which] we forgive our debtors.

We return to our text. Luke 12:58-59:

58 When thou goest with thine adversary to the magistrate, as thou art in the way, give diligence that thou mayest be delivered from him; lest he hale thee to the judge, and the judge deliver thee to the officer, and the officer cast thee into prison.

59 I tell thee, thou shalt not depart thence, till thou hast paid the very last mite.

15

Luke 13

Legalism creeps in unawares. People begin to strive among themselves to attain perfection. Usually, they call out the failure of others to elevate themselves. The following sounds like a legalistic question concerning sacrifices. Luke 13:1-3:

1 **There were present at that season some that told him of the Galilaeans, whose blood Pilate had mingled with their sacrifices.**

2 **And Jesus answering said unto them, Suppose ye that these Galilaeans were sinners above all the Galilaeans, because they suffered such things?**

3 **I tell you, Nay: but, except ye repent, ye shall all likewise perish.**

Jesus gives a similar example. Verses 4-5:

> 4 Or [consider] those eighteen [men], upon whom the tower in Siloam fell, and slew them, think ye that they were sinners above all men that dwelt in Jerusalem?
>
> 5 I tell you, Nay: but, except ye repent, ye shall all likewise perish.

There is only one thing that can save the Jews. Each believer must repent of their own sin.

Jesus continues to teach using a parable. Verses 6-7:

> 6 He spake also this parable; A certain man had a fig tree planted in his vineyard; and he came and sought fruit thereon, and found none.
>
> 7 Then said he unto the dresser of his vineyard, Behold, these three years I come seeking fruit on this fig tree, and find none: cut it down; why cumbereth it the ground?

The word "cumbereth" is like encumber which

means "to obstruct, retard, or hinder." Jesus remained in Israel for three years. He continually sought the fruit of faith and obedience. Verses 8-9:

> 8 **And he answering said unto him, Lord, let it alone this year also, till I shall dig about it, and dung it:**

> 9 **And if it bear fruit, well: and if not, then after that thou shalt cut it down.**

On another occasion, Jesus was teaching in the synagogues. He saw a woman without strength for eighteen years. Verses 10-13:

> 10 **And he was teaching in one of the synagogues on the sabbath.**

> 11 **And, behold, there was a woman which had a spirit of infirmity eighteen years, and was bowed together, and could in no wise lift up herself.**

> 12 **And when Jesus saw her, he called her to him, and said unto her, Woman, thou art loosed from thine infirmity.**

> 13 **And he laid his hands on her: and immediately she was made straight, and**

glorified God.

The religious leader of that synagogue was present and witnessed the miracle. It was the Sabbath and Jesus healed someone. Verses 14-17:

> 14 And the ruler of the synagogue answered with indignation, because that Jesus had healed on the sabbath day, and said unto the people, There are six days in which men ought to work: in them therefore come and be healed, and not on the sabbath day.

> 15 The Lord then answered him, and said, Thou hypocrite, doth not each one of you on the sabbath loose his ox or his ass from the stall, and lead him away to watering?

> 16 And ought not this woman, being a daughter of Abraham, whom Satan hath bound, lo, these eighteen years, be loosed from this bond on the sabbath day?

> 17 And when he had said these things, all his adversaries were ashamed: and all the people rejoiced for all the glori-

ous things that were done by him.

Making comparison of everyday things, Jesus taught about the Kingdom of God. Verses 18-19:

18 **Then said he, Unto what is the kingdom of God like? and whereunto shall I resemble [compare] it?**

19 **It is like a grain of mustard seed, which a man took, and cast into his garden; and it grew, and waxed a great tree; and the fowls of the air lodged in the branches of it.**

He compared it to something else. Verses 20-22:

20 **And again he said, Whereunto shall I liken the kingdom of God? 21 It is like leaven, which a woman took and hid [mixed] in three measures of meal, till the whole was leavened.**

22 **And he went through the cities and villages, teaching, and journeying toward Jerusalem.**

Some of the people would ask questions to which Jesus would respond. Verses 23-28:

23 Then said one unto him, Lord, are there few that be saved? And he said unto them, 24 Strive to enter in at the strait gate: for many, I say unto you, will seek to enter in, and shall not be able.

25 When once the master of the house is risen up, and hath shut to the door, and ye begin to stand without, and to knock at the door, saying, Lord, Lord, open unto us; and he shall answer and say unto you, I know you not whence [from where] ye are:

26 Then shall ye begin to say, We have eaten and drunk in thy presence, and thou hast taught in our streets.

27 But he shall say, I tell you, I know you not whence ye are; depart from me, all ye workers of iniquity.

28 <u>There shall be weeping and gnashing of teeth, when ye shall see Abraham, and Isaac, and Jacob, and all the prophets, in the kingdom of God, and you yourselves thrust out.</u>

The above verse is excellent proof that Jesus

was speaking to the Jews alone about their salvation through the Gospel of the Kingdom. For those who do not "endure unto the end" (Matt. 24:13), they will see the establishment of the Kingdom, but they will not be able to remain. Here are Jesus' words concerning the end of the Tribulation. Matthew 24:13-14:

> 13 **But he that shall endure unto the end, the same shall be saved.** 14 **And this gospel of the kingdom shall be preached in all the world for a witness unto all nations; and then shall the end come.**

All the children of Abraham will be called to return to Israel from every direction. Luke 13:29:

> 29 **And they shall come from the east, and from the west, and from the north, and from the south, and shall sit down in the kingdom of God.**

The first will be those who are alive at His Coming. Then, those who were saved first and are now asleep, will be raised from the dead. All Israel will be reunited at the resurrection. Verse 30:

> 30 **And, behold, there are last which shall be first, and there are first which shall be last.**

Not all the Pharisees and religious leaders were against Jesus. Some came to Him to warn Him. Verse 31:

> **31 The same day there came certain of the Pharisees, saying unto him, Get thee out, and depart hence: for Herod will kill thee.**

His reply is to Herod whom He calls "that fox." Daily He casts out demons and heals the sick. Verse 32:

> **32 And he said unto them, Go ye, and tell that fox, Behold, I cast out devils, and I do cures to day and to morrow, and the third day I shall be perfected.**

The word "perfected" has the meaning of "finished, complete; brought to a conclusion." He is speaking about His task that He came to complete for the Father. His destiny awaits in Jerusalem. Verse 33:

> **33 Nevertheless I must walk to day, and to morrow, and the day following: for it cannot be that a prophet perish out of Jerusalem.**

Jesus laments the City of God and its history of rejecting God and His messengers. Verse 34:

166

34 O Jerusalem, Jerusalem, which killest the prophets, and stonest them that are sent unto thee; how often would I have gathered thy children together, as a hen doth gather her brood under her wings, and ye would not!

Forty years after His Crucifixion, Jerusalem would be laid to waste and made desolate by the Romans. The Messiah promises that He will not return until Israel calls out to Him in faith. (See also Matthew 24.) Here is His quote from Psalms 118:25-26:

25 Save now, I beseech thee, O LORD: O LORD, I beseech thee, send now prosperity.

26 Blessed be he that cometh in the name of the LORD: we have blessed you out of the house of the LORD.

Returning to our text, we finish with Luke 13:35:

35 Behold, your house is left unto you desolate: and verily I say unto you, Ye shall not see me, until the time come when ye shall say, Blessed is he that cometh in the name of the Lord.

16

Luke 14

The phrase "one of the chief Pharisees" does not indicate a position in a hierarchy, but a level of accomplishment or respect of the people. Jesus was invited to this Pharisee's home for a Sabbath meal and He was watched intently. Luke 14:1:

> 1 **And it came to pass, as he went into the house of one of the chief Pharisees to eat bread on the sabbath day, that they watched him.**

There was a man there who had "dropsy" which is a colloquialism for a medical condition called "hydropisy." It is "an unnatural collection of water in a part or whole of the body." Verses 2-4:

> 2 **And, behold, there was a certain man before him which had the dropsy.** 3 **And**

Jesus answering spake unto the lawyers and Pharisees, saying, Is it lawful to heal on the sabbath day?

4 And they held their peace [said nothing]. And he took him, and healed him, and let him go;

Jesus spoke to them again. Verses 5-6:

5 And answered them, saying, Which of you shall have an ass or an ox fallen into a pit, and will not straightway pull him out on the sabbath day?

6 And they could not answer him again to these things.

Still unresponsive, Jesus told them the following parable as an illustration. Verses 7-11:

7 And he put forth a parable to those which were bidden, when he marked [took notice of] how they chose out the chief rooms; saying unto them, 8 When thou art bidden of [asked by] any man to a wedding, sit not down in the highest room; lest a more honourable man than thou be bidden of him;

9 And he that bade thee and him come and say to thee, Give this man place; and thou begin with shame to take the lowest room.

10 But when thou art bidden, go and sit down in the lowest room; that when he that bade thee cometh, he may say unto thee, Friend, go up higher: then shalt thou have worship in the presence of them that sit at meat with thee.

11 For whosoever exalteth himself shall be abased; and he that humbleth himself shall be exalted.

The above is speaking about the choicest location at a feast. To follow, it speaks about the choicest food. Verses 12-15:

12 Then said he also to him that bade him, When thou makest a dinner or a supper, call not thy friends, nor thy brethren, neither thy kinsmen, nor thy rich neighbours; lest they also bid thee again, and a recompence be made thee.

13 But when thou makest a feast, call the poor, the maimed, the lame, the blind:

14 And thou shalt be blessed; for they cannot recompense [repaid] thee: for thou shalt be recompensed at the resurrection of the just.

15 And when one of them that sat at meat [the meal] with him heard these things, he said unto him, Blessed is he that shall eat bread in the kingdom of God.

With this statement, Jesus offers another parable. Verses 16-24:

16 Then said he unto him, A certain man made a great supper, and bade many:

17 And sent his servant at supper time to say to them that were bidden [invited], Come; for all things are now ready.

18 And they all with one consent began to make excuse. The first said unto him, I have bought a piece of ground, and I must needs go and see it: I pray thee have me excused. 19 And another said, I have bought five yoke of oxen, and I go to prove [test] them: I pray thee have me excused.

20 And another said, I have married a wife, and therefore I cannot come. 21 So that servant came, and shewed his lord these things. Then the master of the house being angry said to his servant, Go out quickly into the streets and lanes of the city, and bring in hither [here] the poor, and the maimed, and the halt [lame], and the blind.

22 And the servant said, Lord, it is done as thou hast commanded, and yet there is room. 23 And the lord said unto the servant, Go out into the highways and hedges, and compel them to come in, that my house may be filled.

24 For I say unto you, That none of those men which were bidden shall taste of my supper.

The highly respected and revered of Israel's leadership would turn away the invitation to the wedding. So, at this late hour, the host directed His servant to go and invite anyone who would come. Such will be the case with the Wedding of the Lamb.

Another great crowd had gathered around Him and He taught them. The following is sometimes called the cost of discipleship. Verses 25-33:

25 And there went great multitudes with him: and he turned, and said unto them,

26 If any man come to me, and hate not his father, and mother, and wife, and children, and brethren, and sisters, yea, and his own life also, he cannot be my disciple.

27 And whosoever doth not bear his cross, and come after me, cannot be my disciple.

28 For which of you, intending to build a tower, sitteth not down first, and counteth the cost, whether he have sufficient [enough] to finish it?

29 Lest haply, after he hath laid the foundation, and is not able to finish it, all that behold it begin to mock him, 30 Saying, This man began to build, and was not able to finish.

31 Or what king, going to make war against another king, sitteth not down first, and consulteth whether he be able

with ten thousand to meet him that cometh against him with twenty thousand?

32 Or else, while the other is yet a great way off, he sendeth an ambassage [ambassador], and desireth conditions of peace.

33 So likewise, whosoever he be of you that forsaketh not all that he hath, he cannot be my disciple.

This is consistent with the message of not enduring unto the end and losing the reward. (See Matthew 24:13.)

He compares those who do not endure unto the end with the uselessness of salt once it has lost its taste. Verses 34-35:

34 Salt is good: but if the salt have lost his savour, wherewith shall it be seasoned?

35 It is neither fit for the land, nor yet for the dunghill; but men cast it out. He that hath ears to hear, let him hear.

17

Luke 15

In the previous chapter, the host of the wedding feast was having difficulty getting the invited guests to come. For whatever reason, they had self-interests which prevented them from attending. Do you remember who it was that the host directed the servant to go and invite? Luke 15:1-2:

> **1 Then drew near unto him all the publicans and sinners for to hear him.**

> **2 And the Pharisees and scribes murmured, saying, This man receiveth sinners, and eateth with them.**

To these remarks, Jesus responds with a parable. Verses 3-7:

> **3 And he spake this parable unto them,**

saying, 4 What man of you, having an hundred sheep, if he lose one of them, doth not leave the ninety and nine in the wilderness, and go after that which is lost, until he find it?

5 And when he hath found it, he layeth it on his shoulders, rejoicing. 6 And when he cometh home, he calleth together his friends and neighbours, saying unto them, Rejoice with me; for I have found my sheep which was lost.

7 I say unto you, that likewise joy shall be in heaven over one sinner that repenteth, more than over ninety and nine just persons, which need no repentance.

Let us look at Psalms 53:2-3:

2 God looked down from heaven upon the children of men, to see if there were any that did understand, that did seek God.

3 Every one of them is gone back: they are altogether become filthy; there is none that doeth good, no, not one.[!]

God is saying that there are not any who are righteous, but only those who think they are righteous. Jesus directed His disciples to go to the lost sheep of the house of Israel. (See Matthew 10:6; 15:24.)

Jesus tells another parable saying that there is rejoicing in heaven when one sinner repents. Luke 15:8-10:

> **8 Either what woman having ten pieces of silver, if she lose one piece, doth not light a candle, and sweep the house, and seek diligently till she find it?**
>
> **9 And when she hath found it, she calleth her friends and her neighbours together, saying, Rejoice with me; for I have found the piece which I had lost.**
>
> **10 Likewise, I say unto you, there is joy in the presence of the angels of God over one sinner that repenteth.**

The story of the Prodigal Son is one of the best loved parables showing God's heart towards the repentance of a wayward son. Verses 11-17:

> **11 And he [Jesus] said, A certain man had two sons:**

12 And the younger of them said to his father, Father, give me the portion of goods that falleth to me. And he divided unto them his living.

13 And not many days after the younger son gathered all together, and took his journey into a far country, and there wasted his substance with riotous living. 14 And when he had spent all, there arose a mighty famine in that land; and he began to be in want.

15 And he went and joined himself to a citizen of that country; and he sent him into his fields to feed swine. 16 And he would fain have filled his belly with the husks that the swine did eat: and no man gave unto him. 17 And when he came to himself, he said, How many hired servants of my father's have bread enough and to spare, and I perish with hunger!

At this point, the youngest son realized his folly. This is the beginning—the point to which all sinners must come. The next step is turning around and heading back to his father. This is repentance. The response from his father was far greater than he expected. When his father sees him, he starts running towards his lost son overjoyed at his return. Verses 18-20:

> 18 I will arise and go to my father, and will say unto him, Father, I have sinned against heaven, and before thee, 19 And am no more worthy to be called thy son: make me as one of thy hired servants.

> 20 And he arose, and came to his father. But when he was yet a great way off, his father saw him, and had compassion, and ran, and fell on his neck, and kissed him.

The son admits to his father his wrong-doing and his willingness to accept whatever punishment the father sees appropriate. However, the father chooses to honor his lost son with gifts. His is delighted that he has been restored to him. Verses 21-24:

> 21 And the son said unto him, Father, I have sinned against heaven, and in thy sight, and am no more worthy to be called thy son.

> 22 But the father said to his servants,

Bring forth the best robe, and put it on him; and put a ring on his hand, and shoes on his feet: 23 And bring hither the fatted calf, and kill it; and let us eat, and be merry:

24 For this <u>my son was dead, and is alive again; he was lost, and is found.</u> And they began to be merry.

God sent His Son to redeem or buy back the lost sheep of Israel. The point of this story is God's desire for all the lost to return to Him. Jesus continues as there is one other person in this story — the other brother. Verses 25-32:

25 Now his elder son was in the field: and as he came and drew nigh to the house, he heard musick and dancing.

26 And he called one of the servants, and asked what these things meant. 27 And he said unto him, Thy brother is come; and thy father hath killed the fatted calf, because he hath received him safe and sound.

28 And he [ther other brother] was angry, and would not go in: therefore

came his father out, and intreated him. 29 And he answering said to his father, Lo, these many years do I serve thee, neither transgressed I at any time thy commandment: and yet thou never gavest me a kid [young goat], that I might make merry with my friends:

30 But as soon as this thy son was come, which hath devoured thy living with harlots, thou hast killed for him the fatted calf.

31 And he said unto him, Son, thou art ever with me, and all that I have is thine. 32 It was meet [appropriate] that we should make merry, and be glad: for this thy brother was dead, and is alive again; and was lost, and is found.

In this parable, the other son must represent the other believers who never rebelled against the Father and remained faithful to Him. Jesus assures them that they will still receive their inheritance and they should share in the Father's joy for "thy brother was dead, and is alive again; and was lost, and is found" (v.32).

18

Luke 16

Jesus teaches His disciples about stewardship which is taking responsibility for managing someone else's assets or affairs. Luke 16:1:

> **1 And he said also unto his disciples, There was a certain rich man, which had a steward; and the same was accused unto him that he had wasted his goods.**

This rich man had a steward managing his affairs, but he was not doing a good job. So, rich man called him in to make an account. Verse 2:

> **2 And he called him, and said unto him, How is it that I hear this of thee? give an account of thy stewardship; for thou mayest be no longer steward.**

About to lose his livelihood, the steward thinks quickly and, as a worldly person, puts himself first. Verses 3-4:

> **3 Then the steward said within himself, What shall I do? for my lord taketh away from me the stewardship: I cannot dig; to beg I am ashamed. 4 I am resolved [determined] what to do, that, when I am put out of the stewardship, they may receive me into their houses.**

Using his connections with his lord's providers, he goes to each of them to affect a "deal." Verses 5-8:

> **5 So he called every one of his lord's debtors unto him, and said unto the first, How much owest thou unto my lord? 6 And he said, An hundred measures of oil. And he said unto him, Take thy bill, and sit down quickly, and write fifty.**

> **7 Then said he to another, And how much owest thou? And he said, An hundred measures of wheat. And he said unto him, Take thy bill, and write fourscore [eighty].**

8 And the lord commended [praised] the unjust steward, because he had done wisely: for the children of this world are in their generation wiser than the children of light.

Unlike the children of light, worldly children are shrewd and will seek their own advantage regardless of its effect upon others. Therefore, worldly or ungodly servants are wiser being more shrewd. As this steward was wise in a "worldly" way, Kingdom Believers should be wise in a "spiritual" way. Verses 9-12:

9 And I say unto you, Make to yourselves friends of the mammon of unrighteousness; that, when ye fail, they may receive you into everlasting habitations.

10 He that is faithful in that which is least is faithful also in much: and he that is unjust in the least is unjust also in much.

11 If therefore ye have not been faithful in the unrighteous mammon, who will commit to your trust the true riches?

12 And if ye have not been faithful in that which is another man's, who shall give you that which is your own?

Jesus teaches about two masters using the word "mammon" which means "the love or lust for money." Making money becomes a god. Verse 13:

13 No servant can serve two masters: for either he will hate the one, and love the other; or else he will hold to the one, and despise the other. <u>Ye cannot serve God and mammon.</u>

Many religions make growth in attendance and the pursuit of money their goals. They justify the need for money by many reasons. So too, this was a problem with the established religious leaders in Israel. Verses 14-17:

14 And the Pharisees also, who were covetous, heard all these things: and they derided him.

15 And he said unto them, Ye are they which justify yourselves before men; but God knoweth your hearts: for that which is highly esteemed among men is abomination in the sight of God.

16 The law and the prophets were until John: since that time the kingdom of God is preached, and every man presseth [tries to squeeze] into it.

17 And it is easier for heaven and earth to pass [away], than one tittle [a minute part] of the law to fail.

Jesus assures them that nothing in the Law will change.

Here is an important point for readers to remember. Those who follow the Gospel of the Kingdom remain under the Law of Moses. However, those who follow Paul's Gospel of Grace are under grace. Both *The Hidden Gospel* and *Letters To Theophilus* explain this in great detail. Jesus continues by making a point about the Law. Verse 18:

18 Whosoever putteth away his wife, and marrieth another, committeth adultery: and whosoever marrieth her that is put away from her husband committeth adultery.

Jesus shares another parable which again deals with wealth and the separation that it causes between the Jews. Verses 19-22:

19 There was a certain rich man, which was clothed in purple and fine linen, and fared sumptuously every day:

20 And there was a certain beggar named Lazarus, which was laid at his gate, full of sores, **21** And desiring to be fed with the crumbs which fell from the rich man's table: moreover the dogs came and licked his sores.

22 And it came to pass, that the beggar died, and was carried by the angels into Abraham's bosom: the rich man also died, and was buried;

From death, no one can escape. We are told that each person is appointed once to die and then comes the judgment (See Hebrews 9:27.) We are told that both the rich man and the beggar died. There is a Jewish concept of Sheol or the Greek Hades which is a holding place of the dead. Sheol has two parts which are separated by a great gap. The rich man went to what is referred to here as "hell" or a place of torment. Yet, the beggar went to be with Abraham. Each will remain there until they are called to the judgment. Verses 23-26:

23 And in hell he lift up his eyes, being

in torments, and seeth Abraham afar off, and Lazarus in his bosom.

24 And he [the rich man] cried and said, Father Abraham, have mercy on me, and send Lazarus, that he may dip the tip of his finger in water, and cool my tongue; for I am tormented in this flame.

25 But Abraham said, Son, remember that thou in thy lifetime receivedst thy good things, and likewise Lazarus evil things: but now he is comforted, and thou art tormented.

26 And beside all this, between us and you there is a great gulf fixed: so that they which would pass from hence [here] to you cannot; neither can they pass to us, that would come from thence [there].

The following is going to make a point that many should consider today. The rich man has five brothers and he is concerned that they too will find themselves in this torment. Verses 27-29:

27 Then he said, I pray thee therefore,

father, that thou wouldest send him to my father's house: 28 For I have five brethren; that he may testify unto them, lest they also come into this place of torment.

29 Abraham saith unto him, <u>They have Moses and the prophets; let them hear them</u>.

Hearing the answer from Abraham, he protests. They have the Law and the Prophets, but he has found himself here and so will they. Verse 30:

30 And he said, Nay, father Abraham: but <u>if one went unto them from the dead, they will repent</u>.

Consider well Abraham's response to the rich man's objection. Even if Someone should rise from the dead, they will not be persuaded! Verse 31:

31 And he said unto him, <u>If they hear not Moses and the prophets, neither will they be persuaded, though one rose from the dead</u>.

19

Luke 17

Jesus spoke to His disciples about the opposition. It is difficult to know whether He is speaking about people or the powers, principalities, and rulers of darkness. For all are ensnared together in the kingdom of darkness. Regardless, there will be woe and punishment to come. Luke 17:1-4:

> 1 **Then said he unto the disciples, It is impossible but that offences will come: but woe unto him, through whom they come!**
>
> 2 **It were better for him that a millstone were hanged about his neck, and he cast into the sea, than that he should offend one of these little ones.**
>
> 3 **Take heed to yourselves: If thy broth-**

er trespass against thee, rebuke him; and if he repent, forgive him.

4 And if he trespass against thee seven times in a day, and seven times in a day turn again to thee, saying, I repent; thou shalt forgive him.

The disciples asked Jesus to increase their faith. The Lord explains that they need faith the size of a mustard seed which is pretty small. He says that is all they need. Verses 5-6:

5 And the apostles said unto the Lord, Increase our faith.

6 And the Lord said, If ye had faith as a grain of mustard seed, ye might say unto this sycamine tree, Be thou plucked up by the root, and be thou planted in the sea; and it should obey you.

In those days, there were certain expectations for servants. They were to work and do the tasks to which they were assigned. When it came to meals, they were to prepare something for the master to eat. They were to serve the master until he was done eating and drinking. Then, after the master finished, the servant could eat and drink. To do otherwise would confuse the roles between the two. Humble servants were expected to serve and gratefully receive from the master. To illustrate this, Jesus uses the following parable. Verses 7-10:

7 But which of you, having a servant plowing or feeding cattle, will say unto him by and by, when he is come [in] from the field, Go and sit down to meat?

8 And will not rather say unto him, Make ready wherewith I may sup, and gird thyself, and serve me, till I have eaten and drunken; and afterward thou shalt eat and drink?

9 Doth he thank that servant because he did the things that were commanded him? I trow [believe] not.

10 So likewise ye, when ye shall have done all those things which are commanded you, say, We are unprofitable servants: we have done that which was our duty to do.

As they continued on their way to Jerusalem, they passed through the areas of Samaria and Galilee. There were, along the way, ten men standing nearby who had leprosy. They asked Jesus for help. Verses 11-13:

> 11 **And it came to pass, as he went to Jerusalem, that he passed through the midst of Samaria and Galilee.**
>
> 12 **And as he entered into a certain village, there met him ten men that were lepers, which stood afar off:** 13 **And they lifted up their voices, and said, Jesus, Master, have mercy on us.**

Jesus responded by telling them to "do" something. Their response or action that proved their faith. But, there was one whose response went beyond faith. His response included gratitude. Verses 14-19:

> 14 **And when he saw them, he said unto them, Go shew yourselves unto the priests. And it came to pass, that, as they went, they were cleansed.**
>
> 15 **And one of them, when he saw that he was healed, turned back, and with a loud voice glorified God,** 16 **And fell down on his face at his feet, giving him thanks: and he was a Samaritan.**

17 And Jesus answering said, Were there not ten cleansed? but where are the nine? **18** There are not found that returned to give glory to God, save [except] this stranger.

19 And he said unto him, Arise, go thy way: thy faith hath made thee whole.

The priests, scribes, and Pharisees were powerful people in Israel and the people feared them. There were some of them who demanded answers from Jesus concerning the Kingdom. Verses 20-21:

20 And when he was demanded of [by] the Pharisees, when the kingdom of God should come, he answered them and said, The kingdom of God cometh not with observation:

21 Neither shall they say, Lo [look] here! or, lo [look] there! for, behold, the kingdom of God is within you.

This was not the answer they wanted as it was a spiritual answer and it left them perplexed.

Speaking to His disciples, He reminds them that the Messiah is with them in person. However, that would not last much longer. People will search for Him, but He will not be found. Verses 22-29:

> 22 And he said unto the disciples, The days will come, when ye shall desire to see one of the days of the Son of man, and ye shall not see it.

> 23 And they shall say to you, See here; or, see there: go not after them, nor follow them. 24 For as the lightning, that lighteneth out of the one part under heaven, shineth unto the other part under heaven; so shall also the Son of man be in his day.

> 25 But first must he suffer [endure] many things, and be rejected of [by] this generation.

> 26 And as it was in the days of Noe [Noah], so shall it be also in the days of the Son of man. 27 They did eat, they drank, they married wives, they were given in marriage, until the day that Noe entered into the ark, and the flood came, and destroyed them all.

> 28 Likewise also as it was in the days of

Lot; they did eat, they drank, they bought, they sold, they planted, they builded; 29 But the same day that Lot went out of Sodom it rained fire and brimstone from heaven, and destroyed them all.

This material is very similar to Matthew 24 in which Jesus answers His disciples' question, "Tell us, when shall these things be? and what shall be the sign of thy coming, and of the end of the world?" (Matt. 24:3). Jesus makes clear the suddenness of the end. He is speaking about the last half of the seven-year Tribulation. Verses 30-33:

30 Even thus [so] shall it be in the day when the Son of man is revealed.

31 In that day, he which shall be upon the housetop, and his stuff in the house, let him not come down to take it away: and he that is in the field, let him likewise not return back. 32 Remember Lot's wife.

33 Whosoever shall seek to save his life shall lose it; and whosoever shall lose his life shall preserve it.

Most of the time, the following verses are misinterpreted. The following process of separating people is not the Rapture! At this point, the Rapture has already occurred. In fact, it happened at the beginning of the Tribulation almost seven years prior to the time Jesus is describing. The fakes, the posers, and untrue Israel will be removed. Only faithful Israel will be allowed to remain in the Kingdom. Verses 34-36:

> 34 **I tell you, in that night there shall be two men in one bed; the one shall be taken, and the other shall be left.**

> 35 **Two women shall be grinding together; the one shall be taken, and the other left.** 36 **Two men shall be in the field; the one shall be taken, and the other left.**

The following verses concern the location where they might find the Messiah after He has departed. There are certain birds such as the eagle that are referred to as carrion. These are flesh-eating scavengers and can be found looking in the air as their circling notifies others of their feast. We must look at Revelation that describes the final days of the Tribulation. The following only provides a summary and answers our question.

The Apostle John records the great battle between the King of Kings and His enemies. Here is the results of that great conflict. Revelation 19:15-16:

> 15 **And out of his mouth goeth a sharp sword, that with it he should smite the nations: and he shall rule them with a rod of iron: and he treadeth the winepress of the fierceness and wrath of Almighty God.**

> 16 **And he hath on his vesture and on his thigh a name written, KING OF KINGS, AND LORD OF LORDS.**

The Messiah Who has returned to earth seeking to destroy His enemies. Therefore, if anyone seeks Him on earth after He is gone, here is where He may be found. We continue with verse 17:

> 17 **And I saw an angel standing in the sun; and he cried with a loud voice, <u>saying to all the fowls</u> that fly in the midst of heaven, <u>Come and gather yourselves together unto the supper of the great God</u>;**

Again, these are flesh-eating birds and their supper will be the following. Verse 18:

18 <u>That ye may eat the flesh of kings,
and the flesh of captains, and the flesh
of mighty men, and the flesh of horses,
and of them that sit on them, and the
flesh of all men, both free and bond,
both small and great.</u>

Jesus is speaking about a very specific day. Let us look at the text again. Luke 17:29-30:

29 <u>But the same day that Lot went out of
Sodom it rained fire and brimstone
from heaven, and destroyed them all.</u>

30 Even <u>thus shall it be in the day when
the Son of man is revealed.</u>

Again, the next verse begins with the words "In that day." There can be no confusion about what Jesus is speaking. He is about to face His crucifixion, death, and burial. These religious leaders are still asking for proof. I think His patience with them was wearing thin, but His answer is spot on.

He tells those looking for Him on earth where they can find Him. Luke 17:37:

37 And they answered and said unto
him, Where, Lord? And he said unto

202

them, Wheresoever the [dead] body [bodies are], thither will the eagles be gathered together.

20

Luke 18

Fainting often comes from pushing beyond the limits of man. It results from a state of weakness, exhaustion, or fear. Jesus addresses this in the following parable teaching that man must turn to God. Luke 18:1-3:

> 1 **And he [Jesus] spake a parable unto them to this end, that men ought always to pray, and not to faint;**
>
> 2 **Saying, There was in a city a judge, which feared not God, neither regarded man:** 3 **And there was a widow in that city; and she came unto him, saying, Avenge me of mine adversary.**

By comparing the thinking of the worldly, Jesus wants them to notice how this worldly judge makes his choice. Verses 4-5:

> 4 And he would not for a while: but afterward he said within himself, Though I fear not God, nor regard man;

> 5 Yet because this widow troubleth me, I will avenge her, lest by her continual coming she weary me.

Jesus compares it to God Who will also respond to the cries of His children. Verses 6-8:

> 6 And the Lord said, Hear what the unjust judge saith. 7 And shall not God avenge his own elect, which cry day and night unto him, though he bear long with them?

> 8 I tell you that he will avenge them speedily. Nevertheless when the Son of man cometh, shall he find faith on the earth?

Similar to this judge, there were people there who had no need for God as they considered themselves to be righteous. Jesus gave the following parable. Verses 9-13:

9 And he spake this parable unto certain which trusted in themselves that they were righteous, and despised others:

10 Two men went up into the temple to pray; the one a Pharisee, and the other a publican. 11 The Pharisee stood and prayed thus with himself, God, I thank thee, that I am not as other men are, extortioners, unjust, adulterers, or even as this publican. 12 I fast twice in the week, I give tithes of all that I possess.

13 And the publican, standing afar off, would not lift up so much as his eyes unto heaven, but smote upon his breast, saying, God be merciful to me a sinner.

Each man looked upon himself differently, but the one who humbled himself, God would lift him up. Verse 14:

14 I tell you, this man went down to his house justified rather than the other: for every one that exalteth himself shall be abased; and he that humbleth himself shall be exalted.

Kingdom Believers are to rely upon God and humble

themselves before Him. Certainly, this message will change later on, right? No, it remains the same. The Apostle James would later write to the Kingdom Believers, "Humble yourselves in the sight of the Lord, and he shall lift you up" (Jas. 4:10). The Gospel of the Kingdom and its teachings remain the same until the Messiah's Coming.

Parents wanted Jesus to bless and lay His hand upon their children. The disciples did not consider that an important part of Jesus' mission. He chastised because those who will enter the Kingdom must be like these little children. Verses 15-17

> 15 **And they brought unto him also infants, that he would touch them: but when his disciples saw it, they rebuked them.**
>
> 16 **But Jesus called them unto him, and said, Suffer [Allow] little children to come unto me, and forbid them not: for of such is the kingdom of God.**
>
> 17 **Verily I say unto you, Whosoever shall not receive the kingdom of God as a little child shall in no wise [way] enter therein.**

A rich, young ruler came to Jesus. He asked Him what he must do to inherit eternal life. (See also Matt. 19:16-22.) Verses 18-23:

18 **And a certain ruler asked him, saying, Good Master, what shall I do to inherit eternal life?**

19 **And Jesus said unto him, Why callest thou me good? none is good, save [except] one, that is, God. 20 Thou knowest the commandments, Do not commit adultery, Do not kill, Do not steal, Do not bear false witness, Honour thy father and thy mother. 21 And he said, All these have I kept from my youth up.**

22 **Now when Jesus heard these things, he said unto him, Yet lackest thou one thing: sell all that thou hast, and distribute unto the poor, and thou shalt have treasure in heaven: and come, follow me.**

23 **And when he heard this, he was very sorrowful: for he was very rich.**

As the ruler walked away in sorrow, Jesus turned to the crowd who had overheard their discussion. Verses 24-25:

> 24 And when Jesus saw that he was very sorrowful, he said, How hardly shall they that have riches enter into the kingdom of God!

> 25 For it is easier for a camel to go through a needle's eye, than for a rich man to enter into the kingdom of God.

Those who heard this questioned among themselves who is it that can be saved? Verses 26-27:

> 26 And they that heard it said, Who then can be saved? 27 And he said, The things which are impossible with men are possible with God.

The answer remains the same. When man faints, he must lean on God, His strength, and His understanding. Why is that? "The things which are impossible with men are possible with God[!]" (v. 27).

When Jesus was walking with His disciples, a discussion arose among them concerning what they might receive. They had left everything and followed Him. Verses 28-30:

210

28 Then Peter said, Lo, we have left all, and followed thee.

29 And he said unto them, Verily I say unto you, There is no man that hath left house, or parents, or brethren, or wife, or children, for the kingdom of God's sake, **30** Who shall not receive manifold [many] more in this present time, and in the world to come life everlasting.

At this point, Jesus took the Twelve aside to speak with them openly. They needed to understand what was going to happen in the immediate future. He wanted them to be prepared and know that all this must happen to fulfill His mission. Verses 31-34:

31 Then he took unto him the twelve, and said unto them, Behold, we go up to Jerusalem, and all things that are written by the prophets concerning the Son of man shall be accomplished.

32 For he shall be delivered unto the Gentiles, and shall be mocked, and spitefully entreated, and spitted on: **33** And they shall scourge him, and put him to death: and the third day he shall rise again.

34 And they understood none of these things: and this saying was hid from them, neither knew they the things which were spoken.

For three years these Twelve had remained with Him constantly. Whatever they envisioned concerning the future, it certainly was not what Jesus had just told them. So foreign was it to their thinking that they did not understand it at all.

As they resumed their journey, they approached a city. A blind beggar heard that it was Jesus walking by. Notice that he calls "Jesus, thou Son of David" (v. 38). Verses 35-39:

35 And it came to pass, that as he was come nigh unto Jericho, a certain blind man sat by the way side begging:

36 And hearing the multitude pass by, he asked what it meant. 37 And they told him, that Jesus of Nazareth passeth by. 38 And he cried, saying, Jesus, thou <u>Son of David</u>, have mercy on me.

39 And they which went before rebuked him, that he should hold his peace: but he cried so much the more, Thou <u>Son of</u>

David, have mercy on me.

I believe that it was an important proclamation to those who were listening. Jesus was on His way to Jerusalem for His appointed destiny. This man was acknowledging that Jesus was the Anointed One, the Messiah, and the Son of David Who would be King.

Jesus stopped and asked that he be brought to Him. Verses 40-43:

> 40 **And Jesus stood, and commanded him to be brought unto him: and when he was come near, he asked him,** 41 **Saying, What wilt thou that I shall do unto thee? And he said, Lord, that I may receive my sight.**

> 42 **And Jesus said unto him, Receive thy sight: thy faith hath saved thee.** 43 **And immediately he received his sight, and followed him, glorifying God: and all the people, when they saw it, gave praise unto God.**

21

Luke 19

Continuing their journey to Jerusalem, they entered Jericho where they met Zacchaeus who was a wealth tax collector. Having heard of this Jesus, he was curious to know more about him. Luke 19:1-3:

> 1 And Jesus entered and passed through Jericho. 2 And, behold, there was a man named Zacchaeus, which was the chief among the publicans, and he was rich. 3 And he sought to see Jesus who he was; and could not for the press [crowd], because he was little of stature [short].

He ran ahead and sat in a tree. Verse 4:

> 4 And he ran before [ahead], and climbed up into a sycomore tree to see him: for he was to pass that way.

Zacchaeus had never met Jesus, yet something odd happened. Verses 5-6:

> 5 And when Jesus came to the place, he looked up, and saw him, and said unto him, Zacchaeus, make haste, and come down; for to day I must abide at thy house. 6 And he made haste, and came down, and received him joyfully.

Again, Zacchaeus was a publican and viewed poorly by the people. Verses 7-10:

> 7 And when they saw it, they all murmured, saying, That he was gone to be [a] guest with a man that is a sinner. 8 And Zacchaeus stood, and said unto the Lord; Behold, Lord, the half of my goods I give to the poor; and if I have taken any thing from any man by false accusation, I restore him fourfold.
>
> 9 And Jesus said unto him, This day is salvation come to this house, forsomuch as he also is a son of Abraham.
>
> 10 For <u>the Son of man is come to seek and to save that which was lost.</u>

Observing the crowd and knowing their thoughts, Jesus taught them about the coming Kingdom. Many believed that it would appear before them. Jesus told this parable. Verses 11-24:

11 And as they heard these things, he added and spake a parable, because he was nigh [near] to Jerusalem, and because they thought that <u>the kingdom of God</u> should immediately appear.

12 He said therefore, A certain nobleman went into a far country to receive for himself a kingdom, and to return. 13 And he called his ten servants, and delivered them ten pounds, and said unto them, Occupy till I come.

14 But his citizens hated him, and sent a message after him, saying, We will not have this man to reign over us.

15 And it came to pass, that when he was returned, having received the kingdom, then he commanded these servants to be called unto him, to whom he had given the money, that he might know how much every man had gained by trading.

16 Then came the first, saying, Lord, thy pound hath gained ten pounds. 17 And he said unto him, Well, thou good servant: because thou hast been faithful in a very little, have thou authority over ten cities.

18 And the second came, saying, Lord, thy pound hath gained five pounds. 19 And he said likewise to him, Be thou also over five cities.

20 And another came, saying, Lord, behold, here is thy pound, which I have kept laid up in a napkin: 21 For I feared thee, because thou art an austere man: thou takest up that thou layedst not down, and reapest that thou didst not sow.

22 And he saith unto him, Out of thine own mouth will I judge thee, thou wicked servant. Thou knewest that I was an austere man, taking up that I laid not down, and reaping that I did not sow: 23 Wherefore then gavest not thou my money into the bank, that at my coming I might have required mine own with usury [interest]?

24 And he said unto them that stood by, Take from him the pound, and give it to him that hath ten pounds.

The other servants questioned the Lord. Why would he give the pound to someone who already had ten? The Lord responded to them with this explanation. Verses 25-26:

25 (And they said unto him, Lord, he hath ten pounds.)

26 For I say unto you, That unto every one which hath shall be given; and from him that hath not, even that he hath shall be taken away from him.

There still remained the issue of those citizens who hated the Lord and sent a message to him saying, "We will not have this man to reign over us" (v. 14). Notice how the Lord deals with them. Verse 27:

27 But those mine enemies, which would not that I should reign over them, bring [them] hither, and slay them before me.

This was prophetic! Jesus was now going up to Jerusalem where the rebellious servants had control of

Israel. They too were saying, "We will not have this man to reign over us!" Verse 28:

> 28 And when he had thus spoken, he went before [on], ascending up to Jerusalem.

With Jesus now under two miles to Jerusalem, He would need to prepare for His entrance into the City of Peace. Verses 29-31:

> 29 And it came to pass, when he was come nigh [near] to Bethphage and Bethany, at the mount called the mount of Olives, he sent two of his disciples,

> 30 Saying, Go ye into the village over against you; in the which at [upon] your entering ye shall find a colt tied, whereon yet never man sat: loose him, and bring him hither.

> 31 And if any man ask you, Why do ye loose him? thus shall ye say unto him, Because the Lord hath need of him.

We are going to pause and take a look at two prophets. This event was monumental! Israel's promised Messiah, their future King, was arriving as was foretold by the prophets! This was a joyous occasion and something that Israel had awaited since the time of King David. Zechariah 9:9:

> **9 Rejoice greatly, O daughter of Zion; shout, O daughter of Jerusalem: behold, <u>thy King cometh unto thee</u>: <u>he is just, and having salvation; lowly, and riding upon an ass, and upon a colt the foal of an ass</u>.**

The future of both Jerusalem and the children of Abraham had been predetermined by God Almighty. Isaiah 62:11:

> **11 Behold, the LORD hath proclaimed unto the end of the world, Say ye to the daughter of Zion, <u>Behold, thy salvation cometh; behold, his reward is with him, and his work before him</u>.**

Jesus would enter into Jerusalem. His work was still before Him and there would be no turning back.

As instructed, the disciples entered into the City and found the colt. Luke 19:32-34:

> **32 And they that were sent went their way, and found even as he had said un-**

to them. 33 And as they were loosing the colt, the owners thereof said unto them, Why loose ye the colt? 34 And they said, The Lord hath need of him.

Walking back from Jerusalem, they brought the colt to Jesus. Verse 35:

35 And they brought him to Jesus: and they cast their garments upon the colt, and they set Jesus thereon.

The streets were crowded and people thronged the ways throughout the City. The disciples placed Jesus upon the colt and began to praise God for all that Jesus had done among them. Here was the arrival of Israel's King. Verses 36-38:

36 And as he went, they spread their clothes in the way. 37 And when he was come nigh, even now at the descent of the mount of Olives, the whole multitude of the disciples began to rejoice and praise God with a loud voice for all the mighty works that they had seen;

38 Saying, Blessed be the King that cometh in the name of the Lord: peace in heaven, and glory in the highest.

Some of those present were Pharisees who were appalled by the disciples actions and told Jesus to rebuke them. Verses 39-40:

> 39 **And some of the Pharisees from among the multitude said unto him, Master, rebuke thy disciples.**

> 40 **And he [Jesus] answered and said unto them, I tell you that, if these should hold their peace, the stones would immediately cry out.**

Jerusalem is where Abraham met Melchizedek who was King of Salem. Abraham gave him a tithe of his spoils. The history of this City goes back many years. In this present moment, Jesus beheld this City and wept. Verses 41-44:

> 41 **And when he was come near, he beheld the city, and wept over it,** 42 **Saying, If thou hadst known, even thou, at least in this thy day, the things which belong unto thy peace! but now they are hid from thine eyes.**

> 43 **For the days shall come upon thee, that thine enemies shall cast a trench about thee, and compass thee round,**

and keep thee in on every side, 44 And shall lay thee even with the ground, and thy children within thee; and they shall not leave in thee one stone upon another; because thou knewest not the time of thy visitation.

After this reflection and pronouncement of what would happen in its future. Jesus proceeded into the City. The first stop would be His Father's house. It was time to make it clear that corruption would not run rampart in the House of the Lord. Verses 45-48:

45 And he went into the temple, and began to cast out them that sold therein, and them that bought;

46 Saying unto them, It is written, My house is the house of prayer: but ye have made it a den of thieves. 47 And he taught daily in the temple. But the chief priests and the scribes and the chief of the people sought to destroy him,

48 And could not find what they might do: for all the people were very attentive to hear him.

22

Luke 20

In the week that Jesus would be crucified, He taught in the Temple preaching the good news — the Gospel of the Kingdom. He was figuratively in the "bees' nest." Luke 20:1-2:

> 1 **And it came to pass, that on one of those days, as he taught the people in the temple, and preached the gospel, the chief priests and the scribes came upon him with the elders,**
>
> 2 **And spake unto him, saying, Tell us, by what authority doest thou these things? or who is he that gave thee this authority?**

Before He would answer them, Jesus asked them a question. Picture the people being taught sitting there listening to their interaction. Verses 3-4:

> 3 And he answered and said unto them,
> I will also ask you one thing; and an-
> swer me: 4 The baptism of John, was it
> from heaven, or of men?

The religious leaders must maintain their authority while keeping the favor of the people. So they
reasoned not what the correct answer was, but what
would be their best response. Verses 5-7:

> 5 And they reasoned with themselves,
> saying, If we shall say, From heaven; he
> will say, Why then believed ye him not?
> 6 But and if we say, Of men; all the peo-
> ple will stone us: for they be persuaded
> that John was a prophet.
>
> 7 And they answered, that they could
> not tell whence [from where] it was.

Receiving nothing from them in reply, Jesus does the
same thing. Verse 8:

> 8 And Jesus said unto them, Neither tell
> I you by what authority I do these
> things.

Still in the Temple, Jesus resumes teaching the people by telling them a parable. Verses 9-13:

9 **Then began he to speak to the people this parable; A certain man planted a vineyard, and let [leased] it forth to husbandmen, and went into a far country for a long time.**

10 **And at the season he sent a servant to the husbandmen, that they should give him of the fruit of the vineyard: but the husbandmen beat him, and sent him away empty.**

11 **And again he sent another servant: and they beat him also, and entreated him shamefully, and sent him away empty.** 12 **And again he sent a third: and they wounded him also, and cast him out.**

13 **Then said the lord of the vineyard, What shall I do? I will send my beloved son: it may be they will reverence him when they see him.**

The religious leaders were still listening to Him. I wonder if they knew He was speaking about them?

Jesus continues with the parable. Verses 14-15:

14 But when the husbandmen saw him, they reasoned among themselves, saying, This is the heir: come, let us kill him, that the inheritance may be ours.

15 So they cast him out of the vineyard, and killed him. What therefore shall the lord of the vineyard do unto them?

I am sure this was a rhetorical question as He was certainly not expecting a response from the religious leaders. He tells them what will happen to them. Verse 16:

16 He shall come and destroy these husbandmen, and shall give the vineyard to others. And when they heard it, they said, God forbid.

At this point, I picture Jesus looking directly at these religious leaders as they know the verse in Psalms 118:22. Verse 17:

17 And he beheld them, and said, What is this then that is written, The stone which the builders rejected, the same is become the head of the corner?

Jesus adds a prophecy because He is this Cornerstone. Verse 18:

> 18 **Whosoever shall fall upon that stone shall be broken; but on whomsoever it shall fall, it will grind him to powder.**

There was probably some tension in the air at this time. The Gospel of Matthew adds to this. Matthew 21:45-46:

> 45 **And when the chief priests and Pharisees had heard his parables, they perceived that he spake of them. 46 But when they sought to lay hands on him, they feared the multitude, because they took him for a prophet.**

Our text in Luke completes the thought with a similar conclusion. Luke 20:19:

> 19 **And the chief priests and the scribes <u>the same hour sought to lay hands on him;</u> and [but] they feared the people: for they perceived that he [Jesus] had spoken this parable against them.**

From that time on, they had Jesus continually followed. The spies were concealed among the people and they asked questions in hopes of trapping Him. Evidence against Him was being collected. Their first attempt would be to have Jesus speak treason against Rome. Verses 20-26:

> 20 And they watched him, and sent forth spies, which should feign themselves just men, that they might take hold of his words, that so they might deliver him unto the power and authority of the governor.

> 21 And they asked him, saying, Master, we know that thou sayest and teachest rightly, neither acceptest thou the person of any, but teachest the way of God truly: 22 Is it lawful for us to give tribute unto Caesar, or no [not]?

> 23 But he perceived their craftiness, and said unto them, Why tempt [test] ye me? 24 Shew me a penny. Whose image and superscription hath it? They answered and said, Caesar's.

> 25 And he said unto them, Render therefore unto Caesar the things which be Caesar's, and unto God the things which be God's.

26 And they could not take hold of his words before the people: and they marvelled at his answer, and held their peace.

The Pharisees and Sadducees were both highly educated in the Law, but the latter rejected the idea of resurrection. They present an elaborate example involving the resurrection. Wait! The Sadducees do not believe in the resurrection! Verses 27-40:

27 Then came to him certain of the Sadducees, which deny that there is any resurrection; and they asked him, **28** Saying, Master, Moses wrote unto us, If any man's brother die, having a wife, and he die without children, that his brother should take his wife, and raise up seed unto his brother.

29 There were therefore seven brethren: and the first took a wife, and died without children. **30** And the second took her to wife, and he died childless. **31** And the third took her; and in like manner the seven also: and they left no children, and died. **32** Last of all the woman died also.

33 <u>Therefore in the resurrection whose wife of them is she? for seven had her to wife.</u>[?]

34 And Jesus answering said unto them, The children of this world marry, and are given in marriage: 35 But they which shall be accounted worthy to obtain that world, and the resurrection from the dead, neither marry, nor are given in marriage:

36 Neither can they die any more: for they are equal unto the angels; and are the children of God, being the children of the resurrection.

37 Now that the dead are raised, even Moses shewed [showed] at the bush, when he calleth the Lord the God of Abraham, and the God of Isaac, and the God of Jacob.

38 For he is not a God of the dead, but of the living: for all live unto him. 39 Then certain of the scribes answering said, Master, thou hast well said. 40 And after that they durst [dared] not ask him any question at all.

Although they asked no more questions, Jesus took advantage of the opportunity to ask them a question. He quotes Psalm 110. Verses 41-44:

41 **And he said unto them, How say they that Christ is David's son?**

42 **And David himself saith in the book of Psalms, The LORD [Elohim] said unto my Lord [Adonai], Sit thou on my right hand, 43 Till I make thine enemies thy footstool.**

44 **David therefore calleth him Lord, <u>how is he then his son?</u>**

These men of learning stood silent and gave Jesus no answer. So, He turned and warned the people about them. Verses 45-47:

45 **Then in the audience of all the people he said unto his disciples,**

46 **Beware of the scribes, which desire to walk in long robes, and love greetings in the markets, and the highest seats in the synagogues, and the chief rooms at feasts;**

47 Which [Who] devour widows' houses, and for a shew make long prayers: the same shall receive greater damnation.

23

Luke 21

While still in the Temple, Jesus observed the wealthy Jews bringing their gifts. Among them came an old widow who made a meager contribution. Concerning this woman, Jesus makes a comment. Luke 21:1-4:

> 1 **And he looked up, and saw the rich men casting their gifts into the treasury. 2 And he saw also a certain poor widow casting in thither two mites.**
>
> 3 **And he said, Of a truth I say unto you, that this poor widow hath cast in more than they all: 4 For all these have of their abundance cast in unto the offerings of God: but she of her penury [extreme poverty] hath cast in all the living [livelihood] that she had.**

During Jesus' earthly ministry, the Second Temple was in full operation. After the Babylonian Exile, this Temple was built and remained until its destruction in 70 AD by the Romans. I like to point out that this will occur exactly forty years after the Crucifixion of their Messiah. The people were in awe of its beauty. Verses 5-11:

> 5 And as some spake of the temple, how it was adorned with goodly stones and gifts, he said, 6 As for these things which ye behold, the days will come, in the which there shall not be left one stone upon another, that shall not be thrown down.
>
> 7 And they asked him, saying, Master, but when shall these things be? and what sign will there be when these things shall come to pass?
>
> 8 And he said, Take heed that ye be not deceived: for many shall come in my name, saying, I am Christ; and the time draweth near: go ye not therefore after them.
>
> 9 But when ye shall hear of wars and commotions, be not terrified: for these

things must first come to pass; but the end is not by and by [near].

10 Then said he unto them, Nation shall rise against nation, and kingdom against kingdom: 11 And great earthquakes shall be in divers [different] places, and famines, and pestilences; and fearful sights and great signs shall there be from heaven.

Jesus tells them there will be a division among the children of Abraham. Those who believe God and follow the Gospel of the Kingdom will be persecuted and abused by those who do not believe. Those who believe are called "true Israel." Verse 12:

12 But before all these, they shall lay their hands on you, and persecute you, delivering you up to the synagogues, and into prisons, being brought before kings and rulers for my name's sake.

Your testimonies may be required of [from] you. If that is the case, then do not worry. Verses 13-15:

13 And it shall turn to you for a testimony. 14 Settle it therefore in your hearts, not to meditate before what ye

shall answer: 15 For I will give you a mouth and wisdom, which all your adversaries shall not be able to gainsay nor resist.

God will bring about the restoration of Creation. Israel will play a crucial role. However, there must be a shaking out. This "testing" is to determine who is true and faithful Israel. The Gospel of Matthew records some surprising comments made by Jesus concerning this division. Matthew 10:34-36:

34 Think not that I am come to send peace on earth: I came not to send peace, but a [dividing] sword.

35 For I am come to set a man at variance against his father, and the daughter against her mother, and the daughter in law against her mother in law. 36 And a man's foes shall be they [those] of his own household.

True Israel's resolve will be tested. Will they choose to put Jesus first or their own self interests? He continues with verses 37-38:

37 He that loveth father or mother more than me is not worthy of me: and he that

loveth son or daughter more than me is not worthy of me. 38 And he that taketh not his cross, and followeth after me, is not worthy of me.

Let us return to our text and continue with this theme. Luke 21:16-19:

16 And ye shall be betrayed both by parents, and brethren, and kinsfolks, and friends; and some of you shall they cause to be put to death.

17 And ye shall be hated of all men for my name's sake. 18 But there shall not an hair of your head perish. 19 In your patience possess ye your souls.

The soul represents the mind. Believers must remain confident and unshaken in their knowledge of their salvation. During these trying times, each believer must recall all that Jesus taught.

The timeline establishing in Daniel 9 is currently in suspension. All the events which were foretold will surely come to pass once it resumes. After His crucifixion, there are only seven remaining years! I apologize for mentioning something that is beyond the scope of this book to explain in detail.

How does God teach His people? Isaiah 28:9-10:

9 Whom shall he teach knowledge? and whom shall he make to understand doctrine? them that are weaned from the milk, and drawn from the breasts.

10 <u>For precept must be upon precept, precept upon precept; line upon line, line upon line; here a little, and there a little:</u>

Therefore, be patient. It is the diligent student who gains understanding of doctrine.

Before we continue, let me give you an illustration. You are currently reading a verse-by-verse commentary on the Gospel of Luke. Assume you have never been to Paris. Someone gives you a local street guide. A commentary is like walking through the beautiful streets of Paris using this guide. Now, what if you had a map of Europe showing France's position and how it relates to Europe's history and Paris' relation to the whole. I mentioned three books which systematically divide the whole Bible. They allow you to see the overall arrangement of the Bible and how your present text relates to God's purpose and plan. Such are these book concerning the systematic layout of the Bible.

Daniel's timeline provides markers to identify the progress of the seven-year testing. Towards the latter part, the antichrist commits the "abomination of desolation." (See Daniel 11:31.) Backed by a huge army, the antichrist enters the Temple and proclaims himself to be god. To the believers who see this, Jesus tells them to flee immediately. Luke 21:20-22:

> 20 **And when ye shall see Jerusalem compassed [surrounded] with armies, then know that the desolation thereof is nigh [near].**

> 21 **Then let them which are in Judaea flee to the mountains; and let them which are in the midst of it depart out; and let not them that are in the countries enter thereinto. 22 For these [will] be the days of vengeance, that all things which are written may be fulfilled.**

Concerning the last half of the Tribulation, consider Jesus' words in Matthew 24:22:

> 22 **And except those days should be shortened, there should no flesh be saved: but for the elect's [Israel's] sake those days shall be shortened.**

He is speaking about the last 1260 days or three and one-half years. We return to our text. Luke 21:23-26:

> **23 But woe unto them that are with child, and to them that give suck, <u>in those days! for there shall be great distress in the land, and wrath upon this people</u>. 24 <u>And they shall fall by the edge of the sword, and shall be led away captive into all nations: and Jerusalem shall be trodden down of the Gentiles, until the times of the Gentiles be fulfilled</u>.**

> **25 And there shall be signs in the sun, and in the moon, and in the stars; and upon the earth distress of nations, with perplexity; the sea and the waves roaring; 26 Men's hearts failing them for fear, and for looking after those things which are coming on the earth: for the powers of heaven shall be shaken.**

They can look for the Messiah on earth, but He will not be found until after the great battle. Speaking in the Temple, Jesus ends by disclosing the signs of His Coming. Verses 27-28:

> **27 And then shall they see <u>the Son of**

man coming in a cloud with power and great glory.

28 And when these things begin to come to pass, then look up, and lift up your heads; for your redemption draweth nigh.

Before He leaves, He tells them a parable about the fig tree. Nature signals the coming of its blooming. Likewise, these signs will signal the coming of the Son of Man. Verses 29-31:

29 And he spake to them a parable; Behold the fig tree, and all the trees;

30 When they now shoot forth, ye see and know of your own selves that summer is now nigh at hand. 31 So likewise ye, when ye see these things come to pass, know ye that the kingdom of God is nigh [near] at hand.

We need to pay attention here. To which "generation" is Jesus referring? Verse 32:

32 Verily I say unto you, This generation shall not pass away, till all be fulfilled.

It is not the generation to whom He is addressing in the Temple. The generation who sees these signs will be the one! All that He is telling them will come to pass during "this" generation. Not one word will pass away until it is fulfilled. Verse 33:

33 Heaven and earth shall pass away: but my words shall not pass away.

Jesus concludes with these warnings. The word "surfeit" means "to overindulge in food or wine." There will be many snares or traps on the earth. They must be watchful. Verses 34-36:

34 And take heed to yourselves, lest at any time your hearts be overcharged with surfeiting, and drunkenness, and cares of this life, and so that day come upon you unawares.

35 For as a snare shall it come on all them that dwell on the face of the whole earth.

36 <u>Watch ye therefore, and pray always, that ye may be accounted worthy to escape all these things that shall come to pass, and to stand before the Son of man</u>.

Jesus told His disciples, "But he that shall endure unto the end, the same shall be saved" (Matt. 24:13). They are the ones who will stand before the Son of Man and receive their reward.

After spending the day teaching in the Temple, Jesus retired to the Mount of Olives to rest. But, early the next morning, the people returned to the Temple to hear Him again. Verses 37-38:

> 37 And in the day time he was teaching in the temple; and at night he went out, and abode in the mount that is called the mount of Olives.

> 38 And all the people came early in the morning to him in the temple, for to hear him.

24

Luke 22

Since their release from the bondage of slavery under Egypt's Pharoah, the children of Israel have remembered the night of their deliverance every year. The Passover meal is a memorial of that night in which the Angel of Death "passed over" them and God preserved their firstborn. Yet, God's Firstborn Son would Himself become the Passover Lamb for Israel. As preparations were made, the religious leaders plotted against Him. Luke 22:1-2:

> **1 Now the feast of unleavened bread drew nigh, which is called the Passover.**

> **2 And the chief priests and scribes sought how they might kill him; for they feared the people.**

Judas was one of His Twelve and Satan used him as

a means to betray Jesus. Verses 3-6:

> 3 Then entered Satan into Judas sur-
> named Iscariot, being of the number of
> the twelve.
>
> 4 And he [Judas] went his way, and com-
> muned with the chief priests and cap-
> tains, how he might betray him unto
> them. 5 And they were glad, and cove-
> nanted [promised] to give him money.
>
> 6 And he [Judas] promised, and sought
> opportunity to betray him [Jesus] unto
> them in the absence of the multitude.

Judas agreed to look for an opportunity to betray Jesus where there would not be a sympathetic crowd.

Peter and John were dispatched by Jesus to
make preparation for the meal. They found the location as described and finalized the arrangements.
Verses 7-13:

> 7 Then came the day of unleavened
> bread, when the passover must be
> killed. 8 And he sent Peter and John,
> saying, Go and prepare us the passover,
> that we may eat.

9 And they said unto him, Where wilt thou that we prepare?

10 And he said unto them, Behold, when ye are entered into the city, there shall a man meet you, bearing a pitcher of water; follow him into the house where he entereth in.

11 And ye shall say unto the goodman of the house, The Master saith unto thee, Where is the guestchamber, where I shall eat the passover with my disciples? 12 And he shall shew you a large upper room furnished: there make ready.

13 And they went, and found as he had said unto them: and they made ready the passover.

Finally, the time had come. Jesus was eager to share this Passover meal with His disciples. Verses 14-16:

14 And when the hour was come, he sat down, and the twelve apostles with him.

15 And he said unto them, With desire I have desired to eat this passover with you before I suffer:

16 For I say unto you, <u>I will not any more eat thereof, until it be fulfilled in the kingdom of God.</u>

There is a promise God made through the Prophet Jeremiah. It would be impossible for any other group of people to meet the terms other than the children of Abraham! It has to do with the New Covenant which Jesus is about to share with His Twelve. Let us look at Jeremiah 31:31-33:

31 Behold, the days come, <u>saith the LORD,</u> that <u>I will make a new covenant with the house of Israel, and with the house of Judah:</u>

32 <u>Not according to the covenant that I made with their fathers</u> in the day that I took them by the hand to bring them out of the land of Egypt; which my covenant they brake, although I was an husband unto them, saith the LORD:

33 But this shall be the covenant that I will make with the house of Israel; Af-

ter those days, saith the LORD, I will put my law in their inward parts, and write it in their hearts; and will be their God, and they shall be my people.

God said He will (future tense) make a New Covenant. With whom will He make this future covenant? He will make it with "the house of Israel, and with the house of Judah." Like the Passover Meal that reflects God's provision and protection of Israel, so will this New Covenant provide Israel with the same.

Here, during His Last Supper, Jesus announces the New Covenant to His disciples. Luke 22:17-20:

17 **And he took the cup, and gave thanks, and said, Take this, and divide it among yourselves: 18 For I say unto you, I will not drink of the fruit of the vine, until the kingdom of God shall come.**

19 **And he took bread, and gave thanks, and brake it, and gave unto them, saying, This is my body which is given for you: this do in remembrance of me. 20 Likewise also the cup after supper, saying, This cup is the new testament in my blood, which is shed for you.**

Jesus had told them to expect opposition from family and friends who would turn against them. This was the case in their close-knit band of disciples. Verses 21-23:

> 21 But, behold, <u>the hand of him that betrayeth me is with me on the table</u>. 22 And truly [surely as] the Son of man goeth, as it was determined: but woe unto that man by whom he is betrayed!

> 23 And they began to enquire among themselves, which of them it was that should do this thing.

The Gospel of Matthew provides additional information. Matthew 26:21-25:

> 21 And as they did eat, he said, Verily I say unto you, that <u>one of you shall betray me</u>. 22 And they were exceeding sorrowful, and began every one of them to say unto him, Lord, is it I?

> 23 And he answered and said, <u>He that dippeth his hand with me in the dish, the same shall betray me</u>. 24 The Son of man goeth as it is written of him: but <u>woe unto that man by whom the Son of</u>

man is betrayed! it had been good for that man if he had not been born.

25 Then Judas, which betrayed him, answered and said, Master, is it I? **He said unto him, Thou hast said.**

Jesus overheard a disagreement between the disciples concerning who among them would be the greatest. Luke 22:24-30:

24 And there was also a strife among them, which of them should be accounted the greatest.

25 And he [Jesus] said unto them, The kings of the Gentiles exercise lordship over them; and they that exercise authority upon them are called benefactors. 26 But ye shall not be so: but he that is greatest among you, let him be as the younger; and he that is chief, as he that doth serve.

27 For whether [whoever] is greater, he that sitteth at meat, or he that serveth? is not he that sitteth at meat? but I am among you as he that serveth.[!]

28 Ye are they which have continued with me in my temptations [testings].

29 <u>And I appoint unto you a kingdom, as my Father hath appointed unto me;</u> **30** <u>That ye may eat and drink at my table in my kingdom, and sit on thrones judging the twelve tribes of Israel.</u>

Noticing Simon Peter, Jesus calls to him. He tells him that Satan has set his sights on him. Verses 31-34:

31 And the Lord said, Simon, Simon, behold, Satan hath desired to have you, that he may sift you as wheat: **32** But I have prayed for thee, that thy faith fail not: and when thou art converted [restored], strengthen thy brethren.

33 And he said unto him, Lord, I am ready to go with thee, both into prison, and to death. **34** And he said, I tell thee, Peter, the cock shall not crow this day, before that thou shalt thrice deny that thou knowest me.

He now addresses all His disciples as He wants them to be prepared. Verses 35-38:

35 And he said unto them, When I sent you without purse, and scrip, and shoes, lacked ye any thing? And they said, Nothing.

36 Then said he unto them, But now, he that hath a purse, let him take it, and likewise his scrip: and he that hath no sword, let him sell his garment, and buy one.

37 For I say unto you, that this that is written must yet be accomplished in [concerning] me, And he was reckoned among the transgressors: for the things concerning me have an end.

38 And they said, Lord, behold, here are two swords. And he said unto them, It is enough.

Although Jesus never incited violence, this sword would come into play later in the Garden of Gethsemane.

After the meal, they sang a hymn and Jesus desired to pray. Verses 39-40:

39 And he came out, and went, as he was

wont [wanted], to the mount of Olives; and his disciples also followed him. 40 And when he was at the place, he said unto them, Pray that ye enter not into temptation.

There was a heavy weight upon Jesus. The time of his arrest, conviction, and execution approached. He wanted to spend time with His Father in private. Soon, Jesus would experience the Father forsaking Him as He takes upon Himself the sin of the world. He asks His disciples to be watchful on His behalf. Verses 41-46:

41 And he was withdrawn from them about a stone's cast, and kneeled down, and prayed, 42 Saying, Father, if thou be willing, remove this cup from me: nevertheless not my will, but thine, be done.

43 And there appeared an angel unto him from heaven, strengthening him. 44 And being in an agony he prayed more earnestly: and his sweat was as it were great drops of blood falling down to the ground.

45 And when he rose up from prayer,

and was come to his disciples, he found them sleeping for sorrow, 46 And said unto them, Why sleep ye? rise and pray, lest ye enter into temptation.

The Gospel of Matthew records Jesus making this request three times before the multitude comes to seize Him. (See Matthew 26:36-46.) Verses 47-50:

47 And while he yet spake, behold a multitude, and he that was called Judas, one of the twelve, went before them, and drew near unto Jesus to kiss him. 48 But Jesus said unto him, Judas, betrayest thou the Son of man with a kiss?

49 When they which were about him saw what would follow, they said unto him, Lord, shall we smite with the sword?

50 And one of them [the disciples] smote the servant of the high priest, and cut off his right ear.

Jesus did not want physical violence through the use of a sword. However, its presence there and the subsequent healing by Jesus may have prevented a violent clash between these two groups. Jesus was taken without incident. (See also Matthew 26:47-56.)

In the Gospel of John, we gain additional information of what transpired. John 18:2-6:

> 2 And Judas also, which betrayed him, knew the place: for Jesus ofttimes resorted thither with his disciples. 3 Judas then, having received a band of men and officers from the chief priests and Pharisees, cometh thither with lanterns and torches and weapons.

> 4 Jesus therefore, knowing all things that should come upon him, went forth, and said unto them, Whom seek ye?

> 5 They answered him, Jesus of Nazareth. <u>Jesus saith unto them, I am</u> he. And Judas also, which betrayed him, stood with them. 6 As soon then <u>as he had said unto them, I am</u> he, <u>they went backward, and fell to the ground</u>.

The name of God was given to Moses. I am that I am is a very powerful name for the Creator of the Universe. John continues with verses 7- 9:

> 7 Then asked he them again, Whom

seek ye? And they said, Jesus of Naza-reth. 8 Jesus answered, <u>I have told you that I am he</u>: if therefore ye seek me, let these go their way:

9 That the saying [prophecy] might be fulfilled, which he spake, Of them which thou gavest me have I lost none.

What Jesus says is equivalent to "That's enough!" Luke 22:51-53:

51 And Jesus answered and said, Suffer [Allow] ye thus far. And he touched his ear, and healed him.

52 Then Jesus said unto the chief priests, and captains of the temple, and the elders, which were come to him, <u>Be ye come out, as against a thief, with swords and staves?</u> 53 When <u>I was daily with you in the temple, ye stretched forth no hands against me: but this is your hour, and the power of darkness.</u>

Satan must have been delighted. Jesus was quickly arrested and brought before Pilate where He would be arraigned, tried, and convicted. All His disciples scattered from fright while Peter remained close by and observed. Verses 54-60:

> 54 Then took they him, and led him, and brought him into the high priest's house. And Peter followed afar off. 55 And when they had kindled a fire in the midst of the hall, and were set down together, Peter sat down among them.
>
> 56 But a certain maid beheld him as he sat by the fire, and earnestly looked upon him, and said, This man was also with him. 57 And he [Peter] denied him, saying, Woman, I know him not.
>
> 58 And after a little while another saw him, and said, Thou art also of them. And Peter said, Man, I am not.
>
> 59 And about the space of one hour after another confidently affirmed, saying, Of a truth this fellow also was with him: for he is a Galilaean. 60 And Peter said, Man, I know not what thou sayest. And immediately, while he yet spake, the cock crew [crowed].

Peter stayed close to see the Lord turn to look at Him. The Lord knows His own and He told Peter what would happen and Peter denied it. Yet, Jesus' love for His disciples does not change. It was a bitter lesson that Peter would never forget. Verses 61-62:

61 **And the Lord turned, and looked upon Peter. And Peter remembered the word of the Lord, how he had said unto him, Before the cock crow, thou shalt deny me thrice [three times]. 62 And Peter went out, and wept bitterly.**

The men who brought Jesus to Pilate waited for the court to convene. While waiting, they abused and disrespected Him. His claim to be a King was mocked. Verses 63-67:

63 **And the men that held Jesus mocked him, and smote him. 64 And when they had blindfolded him, they struck him on the face, and asked him, saying, Prophesy, who is it that smote thee? 65 And many other things blasphemously spake they against him.**

66 **And as soon as it was day, the elders of the people and the chief priests and the scribes came together, and led him into their council, saying, 67 Art thou the Christ [Anointed One]? tell us. And he**

said unto them, If I tell you, ye will not believe:

Those with whom Jesus spoke had the equivalent to a doctorate in the Law, Prophets, and Writings. Jesus, as the Son of David, refers to a Psalm written by King David. Psalms 110:1:

> 1 The LORD [Yahweh] said unto my Lord [Adonai], Sit thou at my right hand, <u>until I [God] make thine [your] enemies thy footstool</u>.

This is so poignant because Jesus is now addressing His enemies. Luke 22:68-69:

> 68 And if I also ask you, ye will not answer me, nor let me go. 69 <u>Hereafter shall the Son of man sit on the right hand of the power of God</u>.

They made a final demand of Him. Verses 70-71:

> 70 Then said they all, Art thou then the Son of God? And he said unto them, Ye say that I am. 71 And they said, What need we any further witness? for we ourselves have heard of [from] his own mouth.

25

Luke 23

The chief priests and religious leaders continue their assault by bringing charges that would be of interest to the civil authority of Rome. Luke 23:1-4:

1 And the whole multitude of them arose, and led him unto Pilate. 2 And they began to accuse him, saying, We found this fellow perverting the nation, and forbidding to give tribute to Caesar, saying that he himself is Christ a King.

3 And Pilate asked him, saying, Art thou the King of the Jews? And he answered him and said, Thou sayest it.

4 Then said Pilate to the chief priests and to the people, I find no fault in this man.

Their plan was falling apart. Pilate found no guilt in Him and they became angry. But wait! Not only did Jesus speak against Caesar, He also was inciting the people. He is another instigator! And, we all know that the government in Rome hates rebellion! Verses 5-6:

> 5 **And they were the more fierce, saying, He stirreth up the people, teaching throughout all Jewry, beginning from Galilee to this place.**

> 6 **When Pilate heard of Galilee, he asked whether the man were a Galilaean.**

Wait a minute! Did you say Galilean? Pilate now had a perfect opportunity to defer to King Herod. Since Jesus was from Galilee, a territory under Herod, Pilate could pass Jesus over to him. Verses 7-10:

> 7 **And as soon as he knew that he belonged unto Herod's jurisdiction, he sent him to Herod, who himself also was at Jerusalem at that time.**

> 8 **And when Herod saw Jesus, he was exceeding glad: for he was desirous to see him of a long season, because he had heard many things of him; and he**

hoped to have seen some miracle done
by him.

9 Then he questioned with him in many
words; but he answered him nothing. 10
And the chief priests and scribes stood
and vehemently accused him.

Herod hoped to be entertained by this miracle-
maker's. Since his curiosity was not satisfied, he
handed Jesus over to his military for some hazing.
Verse 11:

11 And Herod with his men of war set
him at nought, and mocked him, and arrayed him in a gorgeous robe, and sent
him again to Pilate.

Finished with Him, they sent Him back to both Pilate
and Herod. In the meantime, these two had become
friends. Apparently, they had differences, but now
those differences were gone. Verse 12:

12 And the same day Pilate and Herod
were made friends together: for before
they were at enmity between themselves.

When Herod's military finished with their hazing,

they returned Him. The chief priests and rulers came in again to continue the trial. Pilate reiterates that he has found nothing of which Jesus is guilty. Verses 13-14:

> 13 **And Pilate, when he had called to-gether the chief priests and the rulers and the people, 14 Said unto them, Ye have brought this man unto me, as one that perverteth the people: and, behold, I, having examined him before you, have found no fault in this man touching those things whereof ye accuse him:**

Neither did Herod find any civil law that Jesus had broken. Having said that, Pilate was prepared to release Him. The chief priests must have been beyond distraught. This was not going according to their plan. Verses 15-16:

> 15 **No, nor yet Herod: for I sent you to him; and, lo, nothing worthy of death is done unto [by] him. 16 I will therefore chastise him, and release him.**

There was a tradition in which each year a criminal chosen by the people would be released. What if we dispensed with the charges and had the people choose who should be set free? There was a man named Barabbas who was guilty of sedition and murder. Verses 17-19:

> 17 **(For of necessity he must release one unto them at the feast.)** 18 **And they cried out all at once, saying, Away with this man, and release unto us Barabbas:**

> 19 **(Who for a certain sedition made in the city, and for murder, was cast into prison.)**

Allow me to summarize. Jesus is not guilty according to Herod and Pilate. However, we know popularity is important in politics and religion. They will give "the people" a chance to let one criminal go free. Would it be the innocent miracle-maker or the convicted man guilty of treason and murder?

Notice what happens here. At no point did Jesus commit any crime according to either the Mosaic Law or the Roman civil Law. He remained innocent. Verses 20-24:

> 20 **Pilate therefore, willing to release Jesus, spake again to them.** 21 **But they cried, saying, Crucify him, crucify him.**

> 22 **And he said unto them the third time,**

Why, what evil hath he done? I have found no cause of death in him: I will therefore chastise him, and let him go.

23 And they were instant with loud voices, requiring that he might be crucified. And the voices of them and of the chief priests prevailed. 24 And Pilate gave sentence that it should be [done] as they required.

The sentence was placed upon the innocent Man. It was declared by "the voices of them and of the chief priests" (v. 23) and it would be done "as they required" (v. 24).

Therefore, according to the will of the people, the guilty one walked free while the Innocent was sentenced to death which would take place immediately. There would be no appeal. Verses 25-26:

25 And he released unto them him that for sedition and murder was cast into prison, whom they had desired; but he delivered Jesus [according] to their will.

26 And as they led him [Jesus] away, they laid hold upon one Simon, a Cyrenian, coming out of the country, and on

him they laid the cross, that he might bear [carry] it after Jesus.

Like a parade, the people followed after Him as they were curious to see what would happen. There were women weeping who knew Him and He spoke to them in a prophetic sense. Verses 27-31:

27 And there followed him a great company of people, and of women, which also bewailed and lamented him.

28 But Jesus turning unto them said, Daughters of Jerusalem, weep not for me, but weep for yourselves, and for your children.

29 For, behold, the days are coming, in the which they shall say, Blessed are the barren, and the wombs that never bare, and the paps [breasts] which never gave suck.

30 Then shall they begin to say to the mountains, Fall on us; and to the hills, Cover us. 31 For if they do these things in a green tree, what shall be done in the dry?

There are seven years that follow the Messiah being "cut off" (Dan. 9:26). Jesus stated, "For then shall be great tribulation, such as was not since the beginning of the world to this time, no, nor ever shall be. And except those days should be shortened, there should no flesh be saved: but for the elect's sake those days shall be shortened" (Matt. 24:21-22.) He is telling the daughters of Jerusalem, they are in for a rough time.

Along with Jesus, two other criminals would be crucified with Him that day. The Passover would officially begin at sundown and the convicts would all be dead before then. Verses 32-37:

> **32 And there were also two other, malefactors, led with him to be put to death.**
>
> **33 And when they were come to the place, which is called Calvary, there they crucified him, and the malefactors, one on the right hand, and the other on the left.**
>
> **34 Then said Jesus, Father, forgive them; for they know not what they do. And they parted his raiment [clothes], and cast lots. 35 And the people stood beholding. And the rulers also with them derided him, saying, He saved others;**

let him save himself, if he be Christ [the Anointed], the chosen of God.

36 And the soldiers also mocked him, coming to him, and offering him vinegar, 37 And saying, If thou be the king of the Jews, save thyself.

There was an inscription of the charges against Him written in Hebrew, Greek, and Latin. It was placed above His head on the Cross. Verse 38:

38 And a superscription also was written over him in letters of Greek, and Latin, and Hebrew, <u>THIS IS THE KING OF THE JEWS</u>.

Because the sign could be seen and understood by all who looked upon Him, the chief priests sought to have it changed. The Apostle John records the following. John 19:20-22:

20 This title then read many of the Jews: for the place where Jesus was crucified was nigh to the city: and it was written in Hebrew, and Greek, and Latin.

21 Then said the chief priests of the Jews to Pilate, Write not, The King of the

Jews; but that he said, I am King of the Jews. 22 Pilate answered, What I have written I have written.

The statement of the crime for which He was charged remained unchanged. He was charged for being Who He said He is: THE KING OF THE JEWS!

There were two malefactors or criminals who were guilty as charged and convicted. They hung on either side of Him. The verb "railed" means "to utter reproaches; to scoff; to use insolent and reproachful language." He was completely surrounded as David wrote, "For dogs have compassed me: the assembly of the wicked have inclosed me" (Ps. 22:16). Luke 23:39-42:

39 And one of the malefactors which were hanged railed on him, saying, If thou be Christ, save thyself and us. 40 But the other answering rebuked him, saying, Dost not thou fear God, seeing thou art in the same condemnation?

41 And we indeed justly; for we receive the due reward of our deeds: but this man hath done nothing amiss [wrong].

42 And he said unto Jesus, Lord, remem-

**ber me when thou comest into thy king-
dom.**

It is evident that Jesus is aware of what was being
said. He responds to the man's request. Verse 43:

> **43 And Jesus said unto him, Verily I say
> unto thee, Today shalt thou be with me
> in paradise.**

According to Jewish custom, the day begins at
6 AM and the evening at 6 PM. Therefore, the sixth
hour of the day would be noon. Notice that something supernatural happens. Verses 44-45:

> **44 And it was about the sixth hour, and
> there was a darkness over all the earth
> until the ninth hour. 45 And the sun was
> darkened, and the veil of the temple
> was rent in the midst [middle].**

With Jesus' death imminent, He commended or entrusted His Spirit to His Father. Verse 46:

> **46 And when Jesus had cried with a loud
> voice, he said, Father, into thy hands I
> commend my spirit: and having said
> thus, he gave up the ghost [died].**

There was a Roman guard standing by overseeing the execution. He was a Gentile and aware of what was happening. Yet, he was not the only one who witnessed this and commented. Verses 47-49:

> **47 Now when the centurion saw what was done, he glorified God, saying, Certainly this was a righteous man.**

> **48 And all the people that came together to that sight, beholding the things which were done, smote their breasts, and returned.**

> **49 And all his acquaintance, and the women that followed him from Galilee, stood afar off, beholding these things.**

One man is singled out in the narrative. His name is Joseph of Arimathaea. He was a caring and righteous Jew who also waited for the coming of the Kingdom. He anticipated the need for a burial vault and went to Pilate to secure the body of the Messiah. It is typical for Jews to bury their dead before sundown on the day they die. It is a sign of respect for both the deceased and those in mourning. By doing this, Joseph provided a burial place for Him. Verses 50-52:

50 And, behold, there was a man named Joseph, a counsellor; and he was a good man, and a just: 51 (The same had not consented to the counsel and deed of them;) he was of Arimathaea, a city of the Jews: who also himself waited for the kingdom of God.

52 This man went unto Pilate, and begged [asked for] the body of Jesus.

The Jewish Sabbath begins at sundown the night before and it was approaching 6 PM. Verses 53-56:

53 And he took it [His body] down, and wrapped it in linen, and laid it in a sepulchre that was hewn in stone, wherein never man before was laid. 54 And that day was the preparation, and the sabbath drew on.

55 And the women also, which came with him from Galilee, followed after, and beheld the sepulchre, and how his body was laid. 56 And they returned [home], and prepared spices and ointments; and rested the sabbath day according to the commandment.

These Jewish women followed the requirements of the Sabbath. They would return the day after the Sabbath to anoint Jesus' body. Until then, they would mourn the loss of their Lord . . . and their Friend.

26

Luke 24

The first day of the week is Sunday, the day following the Jewish Sabbath. The women waited for this day to return to the tomb. We can picture them getting up early and walking together to the tomb where Jesus' body was laid. They talked about the stone wondering how they could roll it away. Suddenly, they stopped. The stone to the tomb was open! Luke 24:1-2:

1 **Now upon the first day of the week, very early in the morning, they came unto the sepulchre, bringing the spices which they had prepared, and certain others with them.**

2 **And they found the stone rolled away from the sepulchre.**

This was not the only surprise. When they entered into the open doorway, the body of Jesus was not laid where they had left it. Verse 3:

> 3 And they entered in, and found not the body of the Lord Jesus.

The events which preceded their arrival that morning began to unravel. There were two men standing nearby who spoke to them. Verses 4-5:

> 4 And it came to pass, as they were much perplexed thereabout, behold, two men stood by them in shining garments:

> 5 And as they were afraid, and bowed down their faces to the earth, they said unto them, Why seek ye the living among the dead?

The men reminded them of the words Jesus had foretold them. Verses 6-8:

> 6 He is not here, but is risen: remember how he spake unto you when he was yet in Galilee,

> 7 Saying, The Son of man must be delivered into the hands of sinful men, and

be crucified, and the third day rise again. 8 **And they remembered his words,**

There was nothing more they could do. What they had come to do for Jesus' body they could not. So, they returned to the others. Verse 9:

9 **And returned from the sepulchre, and told all these things unto the eleven, and to all the rest.**

They returned to the apostles who were waiting, thinking, pondering the events of the previous few days. Arriving there, the women began to recount to them the mystery of the empty tomb. Verses 10-11:

10 **It was Mary Magdalene, and Joanna, and Mary the mother of James, and other women that were with them, which told these things unto the apostles.**

11 **And their words seemed to them as idle tales, and they believed them not.**

Peter could not wait. He departed to the scene of the appearance to observe the evidence himself. Verse 12:

12 Then arose Peter, and ran unto the sepulchre; and stooping down, he beheld the linen clothes laid by themselves, and departed, wondering in himself at that which was come to pass.

There was a village called Emmaus which is about sixty furlongs from Jerusalem. A furlong is about an eighth of a mile which makes the distance about seven miles from Jerusalem. Two disciples traveled after the Passover. On their way, they encountered a stranger. Verses 13-35:

13 And, behold, two of them went that same day to a village called Emmaus, which was from Jerusalem about threescore furlongs.

14 And they talked together of all these things which had happened. 15 And it came to pass, that, while they communed together and reasoned, Jesus himself drew near, and went with them.

16 But their eyes were holden that they should not know him. 17 And he said unto them, What manner of communications are these that ye have one to another, as ye walk, and are sad?

18 And the one of them, whose name was Cleopas, answering said unto him, Art thou only a stranger in Jerusalem, and hast not known the things which are come to pass there in these days?

19 And he [Jesus] said unto them, What things? And they said unto him, Concerning Jesus of Nazareth, which was a prophet mighty in deed and word before God and all the people:

20 And how the chief priests and our rulers delivered him to be condemned to death, and have crucified him. 21 But we trusted that it had been he which should have redeemed Israel: and beside all this, to day is the third day since these things were done.

22 Yea, and certain women also of our company made us astonished, which were early at the sepulchre; 23 And when they found not his body, they came, saying, that they had also seen a vision of angels, which said that he was alive.

24 And certain of them which were with

us went to the sepulchre, and found it even so as the women had said: but him they saw not.

25 Then he said unto them, O fools, and slow of heart to believe all that the prophets have spoken: 26 Ought not Christ [the Anointed One] to have suffered these things, and to enter into his glory?

27 And beginning at Moses and all the prophets, he expounded unto them in all the scriptures the things concerning himself. 28 And they drew nigh unto the village, whither they went: and he made as though he would have gone further.

29 But they constrained him, saying, Abide with us: for it is toward evening, and the day is far spent. And he went in to tarry with them. 30 And it came to pass, as he sat at meat [a meal] with them, he took bread, and blessed it, and brake [it], and gave to them.

31 And their eyes were opened, and they knew him; and he vanished out of their sight. 32 And they said one to another,

Did not our heart burn within us, while he talked with us by the way, and while he opened to us the scriptures?

33 And they rose up the same hour, and returned to Jerusalem, and found the eleven gathered together, and them that were with them, 34 Saying, The Lord is risen indeed, and hath appeared to Simon. 35 And they told what things were done in the way, and how he was known of [by] them in [the] breaking of bread.

As these men stood among the other disciples disclosing these events, there, in the middle of them, appeared the Risen Lord. Verses 36-41:

36 And as they thus spake, Jesus himself stood in the midst of them, and saith unto them, Peace be unto you.

37 But they were terrified and affrighted [afraid], and supposed that they had seen a spirit. 38 And he said unto them, Why are ye troubled? and why do thoughts arise in your hearts?

39 Behold my hands and my feet, that it

is I myself: handle me, and see; for a spirit hath not flesh and bones, as ye see me have. 40 And when he had thus spoken, he shewed them his hands and his feet.

41 And while they yet believed not for joy, and wondered, he said unto them, Have ye here any meat [thing to eat]?

Jesus was alive! He was hungry enough to ask for something to eat. They immediately gave Him what they had. As He ate, He spoke to them and reminded them of everything He had told them. Everything must be fulfilled concerning Him according to the Law, Prophets and Writings. Verses 42-44:

42 And they gave him a piece of a broiled fish, and of an honeycomb. 43 And he took it, and did eat before them.

44 And he said unto them, These are the words which I spake unto you, while I was yet with you, that all things must be fulfilled, which were written in the law of Moses, and in the prophets, and in the psalms, concerning me.

Jesus began to teach them that all that was done was

required. He was to suffer and rise from the dead on the third day. And, everything that happened, God had appointed them as witnesses. Verses 45-48:

45 Then opened he their understanding, that they might understand the scriptures,

46 And said unto them, Thus it is written, and thus it behoved Christ to suffer, and to rise from the dead the third day:

47 <u>And that repentance and remission of sins should be preached in his name among all nations, beginning at Jerusalem.</u>

48 <u>And ye are witnesses of these things.</u>

Jesus had been with them three years. They lived, ate, and learned with the Son of God. He was now to depart from them, but with good reason. It would not be until He left that He could send them the Comforter. He instructs them to wait in Jerusalem. Verse 49:

49 And, behold, I send the promise of my Father upon you: but <u>tarry ye in the</u>

<u>city of Jerusalem, until ye be endued with power from on high.</u>

They walked together, as they often had done, until they reached Bethany. At this point, He was taken up into the air until He was no longer visible to them. Verses 50-51:

> 50 **And he led them out as far as to Bethany, and he lifted up his hands, and blessed them. 51 And it came to pass, while he blessed them, he was parted from them, and carried up into heaven.**

After He parted, they remained as instructed in Jerusalem. They continued to teach the Jews in the Temple daily. Verses 52-53:

> 52 **And they worshipped him, and returned to Jerusalem with great joy: 53 And were continually in the temple, praising and blessing God. Amen.**

Epilogue

At the end of each book, I like to include some closing comments. This allows me to highlight key points. We have approached the Bible from a dispensational perspective. When we do this, it is important "not to hop fences." Many people, in order to fit their theology into the Bible, do just that. There is a danger when one tries to assimilate two different gospel messages into one. They ignore the two different dispensations. I understand that this system of interpretation may be foreign to many of the readers. However, when we understand right division and apply it correctly, the interpretation of the Word of Truth is focused on what the message is and to whom that message is sent.

Seeing the Word of Truth rightly divided, regardless of who we are, is critical. People have been dulled into a sense that the Bible is easy. All that one needs to do is listen to someone else explain it. This creates a problem. Is that person rightly dividing the Word into the dispensations or ages. Are they seeing God's Word in the way God wants it presented? Statistically, the answer to that question will be "No." So, how can we know the Word of Truth for sure? This is the crux of the matter. We must test it ourselves. When we read the four Gospels, we must realize that these books are a continuation of the Old Testament. As stated previously, nothing has changed since the prophets declared His Coming! The gospels tell us the Anointed One has come. They record His life, His words, and His actions while He was on earth.

Paul tells us that Jesus' earthly ministry was to the children of Abraham, Isaac, and Jacob. God made promises and prophecies to their fathers in the Old Testament. These promises and prophecies belong to Israel; not the Church as some teach. Since repetition is the mother of learning, I will include the text again here. Romans 15:8:

> 8 Now I say that <u>Jesus Christ was a minister of the circumcision</u> for the truth of God, <u>to confirm the promises made unto the fathers</u>:

Here, the word "confirm" means "to establish the certainty" of the truth of those promises. The good news or gospel message from the Messiah was to be delivered to the children of Israel. It is the good news of the coming Kingdom—the Gospel of the Kingdom!

The promise that God made to King David concerning the everlasting throne will be fulfilled. That promise concerns God establishing the eternal kingdom with His Son, Jesus Christ. He is the eternal King! For that reason, the Gospel of the Kingdom, is delivered to the lost sheep of the house of Israel. It "confirms" the coming Kingdom. Throughout the Gospel of Luke, and the others, this becomes evident.

Truth is never in the majority. In my opinion, the majority of evangelical churches preach the Gospel of the Kingdom. You may hear their clergy use words like "for the furtherance of the kingdom" or words to the effect that "we need to build the kingdom." There is nothing anyone can do. The Kingdom will be established regardless of what anyone does. God will fulfill His promises. The only thing that can be done is to hear the gospel and react to it. Those who believe will be saved. Those who reject the gospel will not be saved. It is by their own freewill that they must choose to believe.

Many evangelicals merge the Gospel of the

Kingdom with the Gospel of Grace which, as Paul says, is not a gospel at all. (See Galatians 1:6-9.) Let us make sure that you aware of the two gospels. This is not taught or known in most churches or assemblies today. It is as simple as the following example. Bobby would take the black bike and Dave would take the silver bike. How many bikes are there in the previous sentence? The answer is simple. There are two bikes. Now, let us apply this to the following verses in which Paul is explaining this to the Gentiles.

If you read the first two chapters of Galatians, then you will find that there was a meeting between the Kingdom Apostles and the Apostle Paul. An agreement is reached between them. Galatians 2:7-9:

> 7 **But contrariwise, when they saw that the gospel of the uncircumcision was committed unto me [Paul], as the gospel of the circumcision was unto Peter;**
>
> 8 **(For he that wrought effectually in Peter to the apostleship of the circumcision, the same was mighty in me toward the Gentiles:)**
>
> 9 **And when James, Cephas, and John, who seemed to be pillars, perceived the**

grace that was given unto me, they gave to me and Barnabas the right hands of fellowship; <u>that we should go unto the heathen [Gentiles], and they unto the circumcision [Jews]</u>.

We know that the Jews are called the "circumcision" because it is the sign of the Abrahamic Covenant. Paul makes it clear to the Gentiles who the "uncircumcision" are in Ephesians 2:11-12:

11 Wherefore remember, that ye being in time past <u>Gentiles in the flesh, who are called Uncircumcision</u> by that which is called the Circumcision in the flesh made by hands;

12 That at that time ye were without Christ, being aliens from the commonwealth of Israel, and strangers from the covenants of promise, having no hope, and without God in the world

The information above was presented for one purpose alone. I want you to know that, whether you know this or not, the Bible makes it clear. There are two gospels in the New Testament.

For me to write a summary of the two gospels

not laying out the context, history, and dispensational boundaries, would be doing both you and the gospel messages a disservice. Here, all I can do is make you aware of the two gospels and leave you to study them further. As a teacher, I cannot fit all the material of a semester into one class. The same applies to the two gospel. These reading suggestions are not self-serving. I recommend them to you because of their content. Therefore, it is with confidence I recommend the following: *The Hidden Gospel: Once Hidden But Now Revealed.* It is a summary of the Bible, from Genesis to Revelation. It lays out the dispensations explaining each of them and their purpose. This is a book for beginners to intermediate students.

Another book, like the one above, is a summary of the Bible seen from a Gentile perspective. It is called *Letters To Theophilus: Are You Ready For The End Times?* This book includes information about Israel, but primarily deals with the Gospel of Grace. Finally, there is a book that is specifically dedicated to the children of Abraham: *The Glorious Destiny of Israel: The Fulfillment of God's Promises and Prophecies to Israel.* It focuses exclusively on the promises and prophecies that God gave to Israel. It looks at the Bible from a dispensational perspective as it applies to Israel. This book is popular with Messianic Jews.

Other GraceWord Publications

In English:

1st Corinthians: Dispensationally Considered
1st & 2nd Thessalonians: Dispensationally Con.
1st & 2nd Timothy & Titus: Dispensationally Con.
2nd Corinthians: Dispensationally Considered
Acts: Dispensationally Considered
Colossians & Philemon: Dispensationally Con.
Ephesians: Dispensationally Considered
Galatians: Dispensationally Considered
Hebrews: Dispensationally Considered
How Am I Wired?
Letters To Theophilus
Philippians: Dispensationally Considered
Romans: Dispensationally Considered
The Glorious Destiny Of Israel
The Gospel of John: Dispensationally Con.
The Gospel of Mark: Dispensationally Con.
The Gospel of Matthew: Dispensationally Con.
The Hidden Gospel
The Seven Hebrew Epistles: Dispensationally Con.

Two Distinct Gospel Messages Of The New Test.

En español:

Cartas A Teófilo
Efesios: Dispensacionalmente considerado
El evangelio Oculto: Una vez fue un misterio . . .

About The Author

Dr. David Alan Greene has over thirty-five years of experience as an insurance agent selling both property and casualty as well as life insurance. During his career, he taught and explained the content and meaning of policies to his clients. Now retired, he devotes much of his time to teaching the Bible.

He obtained his Bachelor of Theology, Master of Biblical Studies, and Ph.D. in Biblical Studies from Evangelical Theological Seminary where he holds the position of Dean of Graduate Studies. He also holds a Ph.D. in Christian Counseling. He has written numerous biblical commentaries and books on rightly dividing the Word of Truth.

*9 7 9 8 9 9 9 8 5 3 1 3 6 1 *